INTRODUCTION TO
Series Editor: Jonathan Solity

TEACHING PUPILS
WITH LEARNING DIFFICULTIES

TEACHING PUPILS WITH LEARNING DIFFICULTIES

Strategies and Solutions

Peter Farrell

CASSELL

Cassell
Wellington House
125 Strand
London WC2R 0BB

PO Box 605
Herndon
VA 20172, USA

First published 1997

British Library Cataloguing-in-Publication Data
A catalogue record for this book is available from the British Library.

ISBN 0-304-33121-X (hardback)
      0-304-33126-0 (paperback)

Typeset by Kenneth Burnley at Irby, Wirral, Cheshire.
Printed and bound in Great Britain by Biddles Ltd, Guildford and King's Lynn

CONTENTS

SERIES EDITOR'S FOREWORD

The 1980s and 1990s have witnessed unprecedented changes to the education system. These have had a dramatic impact, particularly in relation to:

- schools' relationships with parents and the community;
- the funding and management of schools;
- the curriculum;
- the assessment of children's learning.

It can be an extremely daunting task for student teachers to unravel the details and implications of these initiatives. This Introduction to Education series therefore offers a comprehensive analysis and evaluation of educational theory and practice in the light of recent developments.

The series examines topics and issues of concern to those entering the teaching profession. Major themes representing a spectrum of educational opinion are presented in a clear, balanced and analytic manner.

The authors in the series are authorities in their field. They emphasise the need to have a well-informed and critical teaching profession and present a positive and optimistic view of the teacher's role. They endorse the view that teachers have a significant influence over the extent to which any legislation or ideology is translated into effective classroom practice.

Each author addresses similar issues, which can be summarized as:

- presenting and debating theoretical perspectives within appropriate social, political, and educational contexts;
- identifying key arguments;
- identifying individuals who have made significant contributions to the field under review;

- discussing and evaluating key legislation;
- critically evaluating research and highlighting implications for classroom practice;
- providing an overview of the current state of debate within each field;
- describing the features of good practice.

The books are written primarily for student teachers. However, they will be of interest and value to all those involved in education.

Jonathan Solity
Series Editor

PREFACE

The aim of this book is to review some of the fundamental approaches to effective teaching for pupils with learning difficulties and to discuss current controversies and related research in this area. It contains a description and evaluation of current strategies and techniques used in programme planning and implementation, assessment and classroom management, and examines the continuing debate on curriculum development, integration and challenging behaviour. In addition two permeating themes, that of partnership with parents and the impact of normalization, are reflected in each of the chapters. Some of the chapters of the book, in particular Chapters 4, 5 and 7, cover topics which may be familiar to experienced teachers and lecturers who have worked in this field for some time. However, these areas still feature prominently in all our work and for this reason they are included in the book.

It is my firm belief that approaches to teaching pupils with learning difficulties should be informed by theories of child development and learning which are primarily derived from psychology and sociology. Without a sound theoretical base there is a risk that professional practice can be subjected to sudden and frequent changes in direction. There is ample evidence that this has happened in mainstream education and, as a result, teachers have become increasingly confused about how to define high quality teaching. In the field of learning difficulties, theories derived from behavioural psychology have been extremely influential in informing policy and practice. Despite some concerns about the way behavioural approaches have been applied, which are discussed in this book, behavioural psychology still provides a theoretical basis for much of our work in this field. However, in recent years theories related to normalization and inclusive education, the child as an active learner and the psychology of organizations, have had an increasing and welcome influence. This book considers the application of behavioural theory in some depth but also shows how this dovetails with other theories which influence the education of pupils with learning difficulties.

The book is intended to complement other recent publications in this area, most of which have tended to focus on curriculum development or on more specialist topics such as the education of pupils with profound and multiple learning difficulties or on issues related to choice and empowerment for people with disabilities.

This volume should be relevant to all professionals and parents who live and work with pupils with learning difficulties including teachers, support workers, classroom assistants, lecturers in institutions of higher education, psychologists and speech therapists. It will also be relevant for teachers in mainstream schools who are interested in working in this area and for those who are on training courses.

Throughout the book the term 'pupils with learning difficulties' is used to refer to the group of pupils with whom we are concerned. Essentially I am using this term to refer to pupils who tend to be labelled as having moderate, severe or profound learning difficulties (MLD, SLD and PMLD). The phrase 'learning difficulties' has been used for a number of reasons. First, almost all the areas covered in the book refer to all three groups of pupils. Second, the term reflects a more inclusive philosophy regarding the education of these pupils. Third, the phrase 'learning difficulties' is used in almost all other recent publications in this field. Fourth, the related term 'learning disabilities' is now applied universally in the adult field. Occasionally the content of a particular chapter refers to one specific group of pupils and on these occasions the particular group in question is identified.

I hope this book will stimulate interest and discussion among professionals and parents working with pupils with learning difficulties and that it will raise knowledge and awareness which will inform and improve professional practice.

Peter Farrell
February 1997

ACKNOWLEDGEMENTS

First of all I would like to thank the pupils with learning difficulties, their families and teachers who have helped to shape and challenge my ideas in the past fifteen years; in particular the staff and pupils at the Birches School, Manchester, have been a continual source of inspiration.

I owe a huge debt of gratitude to Professor Peter Mittler who has supported, encouraged and guided me since I joined the Department of Education at Manchester University many years ago.

Thanks must also be given to Jonathan Solity for asking me to write the book in the first place, and for offering guidance and encouragement at a time when the task of completing it was looking increasingly daunting.

Finally I would like to mention my family who have stood by me in recent months during the completion of the final chapters and have accepted the sacrifice of not having a holiday with good grace. Without their support it would have been difficult to complete the work.

CHAPTER 1

Introduction

We begin this introductory chapter with a review of some of the problems in arriving at a satisfactory definition of the term 'pupils with learning difficulties'. This should help the reader understand the nature of the difficulties experienced by these pupils, their parents, teachers and other professionals who live and work with them. This is followed by a discussion of two overarching themes which permeate all aspects of our work in this area and which are reflected in each of the chapters of this book. These two themes are the principles of normalization and associated developments in self-advocacy and the importance of working with parents as partners in the process of education and development. Towards the end of the chapter we consider the potential impact of the recent report of the Special Educational Needs Training Consortium (SENTC, 1996) and we conclude with a discussion of the overall aims and scope of this book.

DEFINING 'LEARNING DIFFICULTIES'
Problems with categories and labels

It is extremely difficult to arrive at an accurate and fully understood definition of any term or label which is used to describe a group of people who are thought to share common characteristics. What, for example, do we mean by the term 'gifted' or 'dyslexia' and what are the consequences for children and families if such labels have been attached to them. Researchers and teachers have spent many hours and written countless books and articles which consider these issues in great depth. Problems in arriving at clear definitions of handicap led to the government, through the 1981 Education Act, to adopt the Warnock Report's recommendation to abolish categories of handicap and to describe pupils with special educational needs (SEN) simply as having a 'learning difficulty'. This group of children could comprise up to 20 per cent of pupils age 0–19. The 1993 Education Act, which replaced the 1981 Act, has retained this definition of SEN.

In reality, however, the delivery of SEN services in the UK is still organized on a categorical basis. Indeed this is encouraged in the Code of Practice on the Identification and Assessment of Special Educational Needs (DFE, 1994a) which gives guidance to LEAs and other agencies on how to implement the 1993 Education Act. The Code includes guidance to professionals on when they should proceed to draw up a statement of SEN for a number of different 'categories' of special need. These include pupils with specific learning difficulties, emotional and behavioural difficulties, speech and language difficulties and learning difficulties. Implied in this guidance is the view that there are indeed separate categories of handicap despite the fact that they have been officially abolished through the legislation. Furthermore, the appeals tribunals which have been set up under the terms of the 1993 Act to arbitrate in disputes between parents and LEAs, have focused almost exclusively on issues to do with definition and categorization of SEN. For example the majority of cases which have been heard by tribunals concern disputes as to whether a pupil should be categorized as having dyslexia/specific learning difficulties. Therefore government guidance and current practice in the delivery of SEN services still operates on a categorical basis and this contradicts the legislation which has legally eradicated all categories of handicap.

Why, then, were categories abolished in the first place? There are four main reasons for this. First, by their very nature, pupils' difficulties in learning and behaviour are complex. Each child is an individual whose pattern of disabilities is unique. To lump children with similar problems into one category may imply that they should all be taught the same curriculum, in the same way and in the same place. The reality is, of course, quite different. Two children labelled as having specific learning difficulties (SpLD) may in fact require totally different provision and separate teaching programmes. Only by carrying out a thorough assessment of each pupil's individual needs will it be possible to determine what the approach should be and which type of provision should be offered. The category SpLD, like many other categories of SEN, tells us nothing about suitable teaching approaches or provision.

Second, the Warnock Report introduced the notion of a continuum of special need. At one end of the continuum some pupils may have severe lifelong disabilities whereas, at the other end, their problems may be transitory. Fixed categories of SEN can imply that pupils' needs are more permanent. Once the category or label is attached to the pupil, it may be difficult to shake it off even though excellent progress may have been made and the pupil no longer has any problems.

Third, as implied above, categories inevitably lead to labels being used to describe the category. A great deal has been written about the positive and negative effects of labelling. In the area of disability, labels which were used in the past to describe, however inadequately, a group of people with problems, for example, 'mentally handicapped' can eventually be used in a derogatory fashion. As Hogg and Sebba (1986) suggest, the word 'mental' caused people to confuse mental handicap with mental illness. Similarly the Spastics Society has recently changed its name to SCOPE as the word 'spastic' has been increasingly used as a term of abuse. For the same reason phrases such as 'mental subnormality' and 'mental deficiency' are no longer used. As Mittler (1995a) suggests, 'terminology in this field has a shelf life of about five years before it becomes unacceptable'. Therefore if categories imply labels, and these labels are used in a derogatory fashion, then categories themselves should be abolished.

Fourth, it was thought that abolishing categories would lead to more integrated educational provision. Historically categories of disability have always carried implications for provision. In the UK, for example, it has always been policy to place people labelled as having a specific problem in the same setting – prisoners in prisons, mentally ill people in psychiatric wards. As far as children are concerned this was reinforced by the 1944 Education Act which introduced nine categories of handicap and encouraged LEAs to create separate special provision to meet the needs of pupils who fell into each of them. Once this provision had become firmly established there were, and still are, very powerful influences within an LEA to maintain it even though the evidence that placing pupils in special schools provides better quality education than mainstream placements is at best inconclusive. Therefore, as far as the education of pupils with learning difficulties is concerned, the statutory abolition of categories has in fact made little difference to the existence of special schools. This whole issue is inexorably bound up with arguments about integration and inclusion and is discussed in more depth in Chapters 9 and 10.

Despite these powerful arguments against the use of categories of SEN it is very difficult to avoid using language which refers to groups of children as being similar. Indeed doctors and paediatricians see the categorization or diagnosis of disabilities as one of their main functions when carrying out a medical examination. As we shall see in Chapter 2, the diagnosis can often tell us a great deal about the prognosis and whether the parents should have more children. Labels or categories can therefore be very helpful and parents frequently see the diagnosis of their child's disability as an essential part of the assessment process.

It is also in the nature of normal discourse that people use words (labels/categories) to describe groups of people, similar events or objects. We need words or phrases to describe a group of pupils who are experiencing problems in development and we find it useful to use these words to distinguish between those who, for example, may be intelligent but have difficulties in learning to read from those who have more global problems in learning. The former may be termed 'pupils with specific learning difficulties/dyslexia' and the latter may be described as 'pupils with learning difficulties'. These phrases are, of course, extremely fuzzy and tell us nothing about the specific needs of the individuals involved. However, they may help to outline some general parameters of the problems that they each experience.

Defining the term 'pupils with learning difficulties'

In this book we focus on pupils with learning difficulties. In doing so it is recognized that many teachers, psychologists and other professionals still distinguish between pupils with mild, moderate, severe and profound learning difficulties. However, recent publications have reflected a trend, now firmly established in the adult field, of referring to people with learning difficulties as a whole group without breaking this category down further (see for example, Sebba *et al*, 1995; Coupe-O'Kane and Smith, 1994; Rose *et al*, 1994; Coupe-O'Kane and Goldbart, 1996, Carpenter *et al*, 1996). Furthermore the Code of Practice also does not make explicit the distinction between moderate and severe learning difficulties.

The term 'learning difficulties' used in this book therefore refers to pupils who might be labelled as having moderate, severe or profound learning difficulties. We are concerned with pupils who will have a statement of special need and who may be educated in special schools or units or be supported by specified staff in a mainstream school. Problems faced by pupils in mainstream schools who are placed on stages 1 to 3 of the Code of Practice, that is those who might be referred to as having 'mild' learning difficulties, are not addressed in this book.

How then can we define pupils with moderate, severe or profound learning difficulties? Clearly, as the above discussion has indicated, this is not an easy thing to do. The needs of individual pupils with learning difficulties vary tremendously and there is no universally agreed cut-off point between those pupils who have or do not have learning difficulties. There are, however, four separate but complementary ways of arriving at a definition of the range of problems experienced by pupils with learning difficulties which can help us to get a clearer picture of the problems which they experience. These are discussed below.

1. The use of IQ tests and other norm referenced scales in defining learning difficulties.

Historically, IQ scores have been central to the definition of learning difficulties, or mental retardation as it was known in the past. For example Grossman (1983) refers to the scores used by the American Association of Mental Deficiency. These are similar to those which have typically been used in the UK. The IQ bands which correspond to different categories of mental retardation are presented in Table 1.1.

Category	IQ range (USA)	IQ range (UK)
Mild	50–55 to approx. 70	70–75 to approx. 85
Moderate	35–40 to 50–55	50 to 70–75
Severe	20–25 to 35–40	Below 50
Profound	Below 20 or 25	–

Table 1.1

The World Health Organisation (WHO, 1968) has used similar IQ bands to those used in the UK by defining moderate retardation as IQ 50–70 and severe retardation as up to an IQ of 50.

The use of IQ tests to classify pupils with learning difficulties has been heavily criticized (see for example Mittler, 1992 and Selfe, 1993). Many IQ tests were not designed to be administered to pupils with learning difficulties, the profiles of these children is typically very uneven and this is not reflected in an IQ score. The IQ scores of young children in particular are very unstable and may change dramatically over time and an IQ result provides no information about how and what a pupil should be taught. A fuller critique of the use of IQ tests in the assessment of pupils with learning difficulties is provided in Chapter 2.

As an alternative to an IQ score, some definitions of learning difficulties are based on an estimate of the child's level of development on a norm referenced developmental chart. Hogg and Sebba (1986) define pupils with profound retardation and multiple impairments as having a developmental level of one quarter or less of their chronological age. This definition is also problematic as pupils' profiles on developmental charts are often uneven, making an average developmental age score completely meaningless.

Despite their many problems, IQ scores and mental age levels, derived from developmental charts, remain for some a convenient way of defining pupils with learning difficulties. However, given the lack of information contained in global IQ scores, they are of little or no use in understanding or defining the nature of problems faced by pupils with learning difficulties. As discussed more fully in Chapter 2, developmental charts do provide more information about the profile of a child's difficulties and they can offer suggestions for programme planning.

2. *Defining learning difficulties in terms of pupils' curricular needs.*
An alternative method of defining learning difficulties is to state simply that a pupil has severe learning difficulties if he/she attends an SLD or school/unit or has moderate learning difficulties if he/she attends an MLD school/unit. This definition is based on an assessment of a pupil's needs in a whole range of curriculum areas and these are matched to the curriculum on offer at a particular school. For example if the assessment of a pupil indicates that his or her needs could be met by the curriculum offered at an SLD school, then the term 'severe' learning difficulties could be applied. If the assessed needs match the curriculum of an MLD school then the term 'moderate' learning difficulties is used. If the assessment indicates that the child's need could be met with a slightly differentiated curriculum in a mainstream school, then he/she may have 'mild' learning difficulties and remain on one of the first three stages of the Code of Practice and not be in need of a statement. (As stated above, the focus of this book is not on pupils falling into this latter group.) This method of distinguishing between different groups of pupils with learning difficulties does not require the use of an IQ test. The definition is essentially functional and curriculum based. However, it is far more meaningful than definitions based on IQ. By visiting a school for pupils with SLD or MLD it is possible to arrive at a picture of the range of children who attend such schools and hence at a definition of the 'category'. As with all attempts to define pupils with learning difficulties, there are problems with this approach, particularly if an assumption is made that the curricula on offer in special schools could not be taught in a mainstream school. In Chapters 9 and 10 we refer to a number of examples where pupils with learning difficulties can be taught successfully in a mainstream setting.

3. *Defining learning difficulties in terms of outcomes.*
A further way of defining pupils with learning difficulties is to consider what typically happens to them when they leave school. Pupils defined as having severe learning difficulties normally require support throughout their lives. The vast majority will not be able to live independently in the community, get married and seek and find permanent employment. Those with more profound disabilities may

require lifelong support in completing basic self-care skills such as washing and dressing and they may never be able to communicate using speech or by signing. It is difficult to be so precise about the outcomes for people who are defined as having moderate learning difficulties. Hopefully the majority will be able to gain employment and to live independently in the community. However, they may also require some assistance in managing their daily affairs and may also have difficulties in basic literacy and numeracy.

Defining learning difficulties in this way is essentially retrospective in the sense that it is dependent on what the person is able to achieve in adult life. It does not help us to arrive at a definition of, for example, the learning difficulties faced by a young child unless we are able to make accurate predictions as to what the long-term outcomes will be. Making accurate predictions for many pupils with learning difficulties is extremely hazardous, and, except perhaps for those with profound and multiple learning difficulties, should be avoided.

4. The relevance of the age pupils were identified on the definition of learning difficulties.
Another way of arriving at a clearer definition of the term 'learning difficulties' is to consider further the distinction between pupils with moderate and severe learning difficulties by reflecting on the age at which their problems were first identified. The vast majority of pupils with severe learning difficulties are identified either at birth, or in the first few years of life. Their problems are likely to be associated with a medical condition, birth injury or accident – e.g. road traffic accident or vaccine damage. Pupils with moderate learning difficulties are usually identified after they have started mainstream school because they fail to make expected progress in literacy and numeracy. Normally such children do not have associated medical conditions.

None of the above 'definitions' of learning difficulties is entirely satisfactory. Essentially pupils with learning difficulties whose needs are addressed by this book are unable to manage in a mainstream school without the aid of additional support from a teacher or classroom assistant. In fact the majority are still educated in special schools for pupils with moderate or severe learning difficulties although some LEAs have made concerted efforts to include them within the mainstream sector. The range of abilities varies from pupils whose only problems are in literacy and numeracy to those who have major disabilities in communication, physical and self-care skills and who may be functioning below the one-year level of development.

As Mittler (1995) suggests, it is difficult to obtain an accurate picture of the numbers of pupils who are defined as having learning difficulties. In the early 1990s he reported that 24,000 pupils were attending schools for children with severe learning difficulties (Mittler, 1991). One would expect the numbers of children attending MLD provision to be approximately double that figure. In percentage terms this amounts to around 1 per cent to 1.5 per cent of the population.

THE IMPACT OF NORMALIZATION

There is no doubt that the principles of normalization, first introduced by Wolfensberger (1972), have had a profound impact on the delivery of services to people with disabilities and to vulnerable groups within society. However, normalization has not been without controversy. Definitions of the concept have changed and the implementation of some of the key principles has been the subject of heated discussions between parents, teachers and other professionals. In this section we shall attempt to arrive at a definition of normalization and we shall review the nature of its impact on the delivery of services for pupils with learning difficulties. A more detailed analysis of the issues is provided by Farrell (1995).

Definitions of normalization

According to Emerson (1992) many countries have adopted different approaches to the definition of normalization. At the outset, for example, Scandinavian countries emphasised the rights of people with learning disabilities to self-determination and to experience a normal life. More recently North American approaches have stressed the importance of total social integration within society.

Problems in arriving at a satisfactory definition of normalization led Wolfensberger (1983) to re-evaluate the theory and propose a new term, 'Social Role Valorisation', or SRV. In this paper Wolfensberger makes the point that the degree to which people are integrated into a society depends on the extent to which they are members of a valued group. In Western societies people who, for example, have a job, are well educated, live in their own house and who are financially secure tend to be valued as being successful members of society. Indeed the whole process of education is aimed at helping them to achieve these goals. Being valued means being accepted as a worthwhile person with associated rights and opportunities to take a full and active part in society. On the other hand, people without jobs, or who are mentally ill, or who have a disability, do not hold valued positions in society and, as a result, they are denied access to many of the every-day choices and opportunities that are available to most people. The philosophy behind normalization is therefore one of striving to give *all* members of society a valued role, where people can genuinely make choices about where they live and how they spend their leisure time and where stigmatizing labels are not used. It is a philosophy which emphasises a welcoming attitude and approach towards all people whatever their needs and abilities.

In translating this philosophy into practice, normalization has two main components. First, as O'Brien (1987) has stated, it identifies the aims of services in terms of ensuring people's:

- presence in normal everyday community settings;
- participation in the social life of their communities and the types of ordinary activities which define community living;
- autonomy in relation to making decisions about their lives in both small and large ways;
- growing competence in acquiring skills and abilities which are meaningful and functional in their lives;
- dignity and respect.

Second, normalization suggests that the means we use to achieve these aims should be as similar as possible to those used with all members of society. In particular, normalization draws attention to the ways in which the methods we use may – if they are unusual – have the effect of advertising people's disabilities and consequently promote damaging expectations among people who interact with them. For example, using pre-school materials to teach adolescents with learning difficulties may have an unwitting effect of portraying these students as being more disabled than they are, with the conse-quent effect on lowering people's expectations of what they might be expected to achieve. Much of normalization is concerned with work-ing with people in a way which creates positive expectations among those with whom they come into contact.

The impact of normalization on services for pupils with learning difficulties

In spite of the voluminous literature on the impact of normalization in different countries and on services for different client groups, its impact on services for pupils with learning difficulties could be described as quite limited. This may be because, in some respects, *all children* with and without disabilities are members of a devalued and disempowered group in society. As we have seen, two key principles of normalization are, first, allowing people autonomy in making choices and decisions and, second, working with them in a way which is similar to all members of society. As far as children are concerned these principles frequently are not applied. Children have no choice about where they live, where they go to school and what they are taught. Methods of controlling them, e.g. physical punishment from parents or detention at school, are not used with adult populations, as they would be regarded as illegal or an infringement of personal liberty. Hence all pupils are treated in a way which reinforces their status as members of a devalued and disempowered group. As it is in accordance with principles of normalization for pupils with learning difficulties to be treated no differently from their same-age peers, inevitably they will be also be members of this devalued and disempowered group.

Despite this salutary reminder about the limited impact that normalization can have on all children, there are two aspects of the approach, both of which are controversial, which have influenced the delivery of services to pupils with learning difficulties.

First, normalization principles state that people with disabilities should attend normal everyday community settings. This implies that pupils should be educated in mainstream schools. At the present time, however, the vast majority of pupils with learning difficulties still attend special schools and, indeed, as discussed in Chapter 10, there is ample evidence to indicate that there are major problems in providing genuinely inclusive education for all pupils with learning difficulties. Nevertheless there is a small but increasing number of pupils with learning difficulties who are now being educated in mainstream settings on a full-time basis and the vast majority of special schools have developed links with mainstream schools. Integration and inclusion are now firmly on the agenda and, hopefully, opportunities for pupils with learning difficulties to attend mainstream settings will continue to increase. In this respect normalization has had an influence on the provision of education services.

Second, as stated above, normalization principles stress the importance of enabling people to make choices and decisions in their lives and to feel empowered to do so. This aspect of normalization is closely related to concepts of self-advocacy. Although all pupils, including those without disabilities, are denied opportunities to make choices and decisions, there are important implications from this basic principle which can and should affect the way parents and professionals work with pupils with learning difficulties. Many writers (for example Tilstone, 1991; Sebba *et al*, 1995) have made the point that the education of pupils with learning difficulties has been characterized by others making decisions about all aspects of their lives, for example what they should eat, wear, watch on TV, who they should play with. These and other authors criticize much early work on curriculum development as being too teacher-dominated and hence disempowering for the pupils who were given little or no choice over what they were taught. It is now generally accepted that part of good education for pupils with learning disabilities is ensuring that they are given maximum opportunities to be fully involved in planning all aspects of their lives. Mittler (1996a) goes one step further by suggesting that these goals could be achieved if schools and services for pupils with learning difficulties adopted a self-advocacy curriculum. This curriculum should 'inform and permeate each and every activity undertaken in the school and in the home'.

Mittler (*op. cit.*) also refers to the establishment of self-advocacy groups who work together, sometimes with support, to make sure that their voice is heard among professionals and parents. Winup (1994), for example, provides a fascinating account of the establishment of a student committee of 16- to 18-year-old pupils with severe and moderate learning difficulties which focused, in particular, on their preparation for independence. Garner and Sandow (1995) provide an excellent discussion of the issues surrounding advocacy and self-advocacy for pupils with special needs. They also highlight some of the problems which can occur. For example, they suggest that pupils may not always want to advocate for themselves and quote anecdotal research suggesting that the lessons most disliked by pupils were when they could choose an activity. They also point out that pupils may express wishes that are inappropriate or dangerous. In addition McConkey (1994) argues that there is a danger that those advocacy groups which can only function with staff support may end up with the wishes of the staff and not the participants being expressed.

Despite these problems, it is generally accepted that opportunities for self-advocacy in pupils with learning difficulties should be encouraged. However, this has to be seen in the context of normal childhood where pupil autonomy is restricted and where parents are expected, and teachers are paid, to educate and control their pupils.

The impact of normalization on teaching methods

As stated above, normalization suggests that teaching methods should be as similar to those used with all members of society. In recent years two teaching approaches, sometimes seen as contrasting, have been criticized as being contrary to normalization principles. Behavioural methods have been criticized as denying pupils choice and as being generally disempowering, and interactive methods have been accused of being non-age-appropriate. These issues are discussed in more detail in Chapters 3 and 6 where it is concluded that, if applied sensitively and in appropriate contexts, neither approach is incompatible with normalization.

In conclusion, normalization has undoubtedly influenced and informed discussions and debates about the delivery of services to pupils with learning difficulties. Indeed in the Code of Practice (DFE 1994) the government appears to have accepted the philosophy behind normalization by encouraging professionals to involve pupils in their statutory assessments wherever possible. Professional practice has also moved forward in other specific areas such as integration and self-advocacy. However, there are many difficulties inherent in the philosophy of normalization and these continue to be a source of controversy.

WORKING WITH PARENTS

In the last twenty years many books have been published on the importance of involving parents in the education of pupils with special needs (see for example, Mittler and McConachie, 1983; Cunningham and Davis, 1985; McConkey, 1985; Byrne *et al*, 1988; Mittler and Mittler, 1994). Indeed involving parents in the assessment and review of pupils with special needs is enshrined in the 1981 and 1993 Education Acts and in the Code of Practice. However, despite the rhetoric and examples of good practice that appear in the above publications, Mittler (1995b) and Carpenter (1996) report that problems still remain in the development of effective partnership between parents of pupils with learning difficulties and the professionals with whom they come into contact. Marks *et al* (1995) also report on the way in which teachers can, in quite subtle ways, disempower and exclude parents from taking part in annual review meetings as an equal partner.

In order to maximize the chances of working effectively with parents of pupils with learning difficulties it is important to consider the impact that having such a child can have on the family. During pregnancy the vast majority of families do not even consider that their baby may be born with, or develop, a learning difficulty. Typically they look forward to having a healthy baby who will grow up to live a 'normal' life. They may never have met a child or adult with a disability. Consequently the news that they have a child with a learning difficulty is likely to come as a huge shock. Not only have they 'lost' the normal baby they were hoping for but they have also 'gained' a child who is likely to have major learning problems and may need support throughout his or her life. In addition this baby may look different from other children, especially if he/she has a physical disability or has Down's Syndrome, and this only serves to isolate the baby as being different from others. In adjusting to the presence of the new child with learning difficulties, the family may well go through a grieving process similar to that which people may go through if someone close to them dies suddenly (e.g. a mother, son, daughter, husband or wife). These can include feelings of emptiness, disbelief, anger, blame, hope and many more. Carpenter (*op. cit.*) suggests that, for some parents, the grieving process may last for many years.

The presence of the child with learning difficulties therefore has a long-term impact on the whole family. The fact that the baby may have lifelong difficulties and will almost certainly never be 'cured' means that he/she may need to be looked after until death and almost certainly after the parents have died. The parents therefore have a 'child for life' and this dramatically affects the plans they might have for their old age. It will also have an impact on the rest of the family.

As a consequence of having a child with a learning disability in the family, the parents may be offered help and support from a range of different agencies and voluntary organizations. Clearly, in view of the complex needs that pupils with disabilities may have, a large number of professionals could become involved, particularly if the child has associated physical and sensory difficulties. These professionals are likely to include: the GP, health visitor, paediatrician, physiotherapist, audiologist, occupational therapist, ophthalmologist, social worker, speech and language therapist, clinical and educational psychologist, teachers and members of voluntary organizations. Having a child with a disability brings with it the additional burden of having to attend appointments to see the various professionals involved. These appointments are usually at hospitals or clinics which may be some distance from the family home, they require the parents to make long bus journeys and to wait for long periods of time in uncomfortable waiting rooms. There is a real danger that these appointments with the large variety of different professionals may be seen by the parents to be counter-productive. Yet the last thing they wish to be accused of is being an unco-operative and uncaring parent, and so, against the odds, and often at inconvenient times, they trawl their child round the various professionals. On one occasion an educational psychologist was informed by a tetchy and overburdened parent that she was the twenty-second different professional that she and her daughter had seen in the past three weeks!

Parents therefore face a great many problems in coming to terms with having a child with a learning difficulty, in facing the future and in coping with the different agencies who may be involved. Many have extremely unhappy memories of their involvement with different professionals which only exacerbates their problems. It is therefore essential for all professionals to work as effectively as possible with parents at every stage of the child's life. Not only should this help families to come to terms with their child's problems, but it will also maximize the chances that the most effective and valued services will be offered to the child. Parents, after all, know their children best and can provide detailed information about their learning and behaviour which may not be known to others. They are also a valuable teaching resource and can work with teachers and others in implementing specific programmes of work. Work with parents should at all times be on an equal basis, with professionals respecting the parents' expertise and contributions as they would respect those of any other professional.

It should also be noted that, just as parents have a right to be involved as fully as possible in working with the other agencies, they also have a right *not* to be involved. Some parents may, for example, see it as the school's job to teach the child and the last thing they want is to be dragged into doing some extra work in the evening. Many parents may have full-time and demanding jobs and other additional problems that impinge on their lives. They may not normally work with their non-disabled children at home and therefore see no reason why they should work with the child who has learning difficulties. The right not to be involved should therefore be respected by teachers and other professionals.

We shall conclude this section by summarizing the views that families of pupils with learning difficulties have expressed in research projects reported by Mittler (1995b). Families value professionals who:

- treat them and the disabled with respect and dignity;
- have high expectations;
- communicate openly and honestly;
- show sensitivity and understanding for their feelings;
- have a hopeful and positive stance, emphasising abilities and possibilities;
- share information and skills;
- explain their role;
- explain the agencies' responsibilities;
- explain rights and entitlements;
- advocate for better services and more humane policies;
- plan services with, and not for, families;
- do not stereotype disabled persons or families.

General principles of support should:

- always be mindful of the rights of the disabled person;
- be offered on the basis of needs identified either by families themselves or in collaboration with families;
- be offered in a way which is appropriate to the individual family;
- remain flexible, the mode, amount, timing of support being responsive to changing circumstances and needs;
- maximize the degree of control exercised by the disabled person and the family;
- facilitate the integration of the disabled person and the family into the life of the community.

It is important to remember that effective parental involvement is not an additional topic which should be treated separately and distinctly from other aspects of work with pupils with disabilities. On the contrary, it influences all aspects of work in this field and therefore, like principles of normalization, parental involvement is a permeating theme which is reflected in all the chapters of this book.

TEACHER TRAINING IN SPECIAL EDUCATION

In February 1996 the Special Educational Needs Training Consortium published a report entitled *Professional Development to Meet Special Educational Needs* (SENTC, 1996). The document, written for the Department for Education and Employment, highlights the problems faced by schools, LEAs and institutions of higher education in providing adequate training for staff who work with pupils with SEN. Porter (1996) discusses issues raised in the report in some depth. In the severe learning difficulties field, for example, nearly half the teachers working in SLD schools have no specific training to work in this area and the SENTC report suggests ways in which the government could rectify the situation.

The appendix to the report contains a list of core competencies based on the required knowledge, skills and understanding which teachers in specific SEN fields should possess. These competencies should inform course providers. Each set of competencies is designed to be seen as a 'working document' and will be continually updated and modified. However, they represent an important first step in trying to define precisely what a teacher of pupils with SEN should know, understand and be able to do. The main body of the report contains some general competencies which all teachers of pupils with SEN should possess. These include the following:

- knowledge of SEN legislation;
- an awareness of the importance of working with parents;
- knowledge of the role of LEA support services and other agencies;
- an ability to identify pupils' strengths and needs;
- an ability to deliver a broad, balanced and relevant curriculum.

The core competencies in each area of SEN include separate competencies for teachers working with pupils with MLD and SLD. This is unfortunate and contrary to developments towards a more inclusive approach to special needs education and to the ethos of recent publications in this area which have suggested that the term 'learning difficulties' should be used to cover both these groups of pupils. Having two sets of competencies conveys the impression that the techniques required to teach such pupils are different when this is manifestly not the case. Presumably the authors are not wishing to imply that teachers who, for example, become competent to teach pupils in MLD schools will not be competent to teach pupils with SLD. Such a position would be unsustainable on pragmatic and educational grounds.

Despite the fact that there are two sets of competencies for pupils with MLD and SLD, there are important similarities between them which could form the basis for developing a more inclusive set of competencies for teachers working with all pupils with learning difficulties. These similarities are reflected in the following summary of the broad areas of work referred to in the competencies:

1. Working with families.
2. An awareness of the impact that schools, families and communities can have on pupils' development and learning.
3. An ability to assess the needs of individuals and groups of pupils and to plan broad, balanced and relevant educational programmes to meet these needs.
4. An ability to work with professional colleagues, parents and support services in planning programmes of work and in curriculum and whole school development, either informally or in meetings and case conferences.
5. Knowledge of the stages of child development, of problems in development experienced by pupils with specified disabilities and of the implications of this for education.
6. An ability to develop opportunities for integration and inclusion.

This summary of the SENTC competencies only provides a brief overview of the knowledge, skills and awareness which teachers of pupils with learning difficulties should possess. In order for teachers to acquire these competencies, they require substantial school-based experience and training in a variety of settings which is supported and guided by experienced teachers working in the same area. At the present time the government shows no sign of making the necessary resources available to enable teachers of all pupils with SEN to receive the training that is needed.

CONCLUSION: THE AIMS AND SCOPE OF THIS BOOK

The overall aim of this book is to combine a review of existing theory and practice in the education of pupils with learning difficulties with a discussion of some more controversial issues. Pupils with learning difficulties present many challenges for their parents, teachers and other professionals. It is important for all our work in this area to be informed by knowledge and theory, and this should be combined with enthusiasm and a commitment to work in collaboration and partnership with everybody involved.

This introductory chapter has discussed some of the problems in arriving at a satisfactory definition of the term 'learning difficulties'; we have considered two permeating themes which will run through the whole book, normalization and parental involvement, and we have briefly referred to the SENTC report. Chapter 2 considers approaches to the assessment of pupils with learning difficulties and incorporates a discussion of the effect of legislation and role of different agencies in this process. Chapter 3 provides a theoretical overview of the impact of behavioural teaching strategies and discusses some of the arguments for and against their use. This analysis is relevant to policy and practice for pupils with learning difficulties in all areas of school and family life. Chapters 4 and 5 describe and review specific approaches to programme planning and implementation when working with individuals and groups of pupils. Chapter 6 reviews current approaches to curriculum planning in the context of developments which have taken place prior to and since the advent of the National Curriculum. In Chapter 7 we consider approaches to effective classroom organization and management. Chapter 8 covers pupils with challenging behaviour and includes a review of the incidence and definition of challenging behaviour and discusses a range of different intervention strategies which can be used. Chapters 9 and 10 review current developments and research into the integration of pupils with learning difficulties.

Finally it is important to remember that pupils with learning difficulties have many varied and complex needs just like everyone else. Everybody needs to feel loved and respected, to be a valued member of society and to have opportunities to gain access to all that it offers. Ultimately we all should be able, within the law, to choose what we learn and where we live, whom we live with and what we do. Therefore, in all our work with pupils with learning difficulties we should, wherever possible, consult with the pupils and families whose needs we are trying to meet and through this provide an overall education which is designed to help them to reach this ultimate goal of independence and autonomy.

CHAPTER 2

The assessment of pupils with learning difficulties

INTRODUCTION

Over the years a great deal has been written about the assessment of pupils with learning difficulties (see, for example, Hogg and Raynes, 1987; Mittler, 1992). Numerous tests and developmental charts and checklists have been produced, some within an explicit theoretical orientation. Government legislation and accompanying guidance (in particular the 1981 and 1993 Education Acts) have placed the assessment of pupils with disabilities within a legal framework and have also exhorted professionals to work co-operatively together with the full involvement of parents. There is insufficient space in this chapter to provide a wide-ranging review of approaches to assessment. We shall therefore limit our discussion to the following:

- the concept of assessment in general;
- the contexts in which assessments can take place and the professionals involved;
- the range of questions which people ask when assessing pupils with learning difficulties;
- some of the assessment techniques which might be used.

THE CONCEPT OF ASSESSMENT

In general terms the concept of assessment is extremely broad and is by no means restricted to people with disabilities. All pupils and adults undergo many forms of assessment throughout their lives. Pupils are assessed at the end of each of the National Curriculum Key Stages and many also take additional school-based tests. This process continues at institutions of further and higher education. Indeed the results of these assessments play a crucial role in determining the future careers of all students as they enable them to have, or deny them access to, further education and job opportunities. The mode of

19

assessment varies from unseen examinations or tests, to ongoing continuous assessment, sometimes completed by the pupil's teachers, and to 'subjective' reports compiled by teachers and pupils which may contribute to the pupil's ongoing Record of Achievement.

However, the concept of assessment applies to far more than the evaluation of pupils' school performance. All of us are inexorably involved in carrying out assessments throughout our lives. Some of these assessments may relate to our work, for example the driving instructor who assesses whether a person is ready to take a driving test, or the interview panel which assesses the suitability of candidates for a job or profession. Other assessments are less formal and carried out quite naturally. For example parents assess whether a potential future son- or daughter-in-law will be a suitable partner for their child, or a teacher assesses the competence and reliability of his or her head of department. Often these assessments are based on superficial factors such as a person's physical appearance. Indeed when we consult our doctor, our assessment of his/her competence might be affected by the clothes he/she is wearing. If the GP is wearing jeans and a T-shirt, we might question his/her competence – quite irrationally, as there is no reason why style of dress should affect the way a GP works.

The concept of assessment is not restricted to the assessment of individuals. We also assess institutions and groups such as schools and families and draw conclusions as to the effect that they may have on individuals within them. These assessments are rarely made on the basis of a formal 'examination' or structured observation, unless one is an OFSTED inspector or a trained family therapist. All of us make rapid and very informal judgements about schools, families and communities which may be based on inaccurate reports from our friends, neighbours and colleagues or on an unfortunate first impression such as being met by a pupil at the school gate who was unable to give directions to the secretary's office.

It is also the case that we may make assessments without being fully aware of the reasons why we have come to a particular conclusion and, in particular, how our own prejudices might have influenced us. It is not uncommon for people to hold irrational beliefs about, for example, the superiority of private education, the potential for parents from working-class families to abuse their children or the dangers posed to society of relocating people with learning disabilities from hospitals into the community. These assessments, which may be based on prejudicial beliefs, can affect our professional practice in insidious ways and it is vital for all of us who work in the helping professions (doctors, teachers, nurses, psychologists, social workers etc.) to be aware of how our own, and rarely stated, prejudices can affect our judgements. We should also counter the prejudicial judgements of others wherever possible.

From the above it can be seen that assessment is a complex process which affects us all. However, the issues raised also affect the assessment of pupils with learning difficulties as such pupils do not exist in isolation from their families, schools and communities. For example, families may have been 'exposed' to the results of 'assessments' by friends and other family members who may hold prejudicial beliefs about disability or whose ignorance about handicap may have led them to say or do things which have made things worse for the family. Some relatives may have viewed the birth of a handicapped child as being a curse on the family and as a result they are ostracized.

In order to carry out assessments effectively, professionals need to be informed about disability, to have confronted their own ignorance and prejudices, to have received appropriate training and to communicate their findings in a sensitive and constructive manner. This is particularly important as many parents are understandably anxious and apprehensive when their child is undergoing a formal assessment, particularly if this involves many people and if they are required to attend a meeting at school or a child development centre. As we stated in the introduction to this book, many parents have extremely unhappy memories of the way they found out about their child's disability. This can affect their future relationships with professionals who are involved in assessing the child throughout his or her life.

THE CONTEXT IN WHICH ASSESSMENTS TAKE PLACE AND THE PROFESSIONALS INVOLVED

Assessment and its consequences therefore have a key part to play in planning and delivering effective services for pupils with learning difficulties. Assessment is also a continuing feature of these pupils' lives and involves many different people. However, from the parents' point of view the following three periods of the child's life are the most crucial in terms of the impact that the findings may have:

- at birth or on recognition of the disability;
- when decisions about schooling are made;
- when the pupil is about to leave school.

Assessments which take place during these periods may occur in different settings, for example the home, school and hospital child development centre, and many different professionals will be involved.

21

Assessment at birth or on first identification of a problem

If the child's disability is identified at birth, hospital doctors, in particular paediatricians, will almost certainly be the main professionals involved in the assessment. They will answer questions about the name of the disability, the cause, and the likely prognosis. Other professionals involved at this stage could be a social worker and health visitor, and, depending on possible associated physical or sensory difficulties, physiotherapists, audiologists and ophthalmologists. At this early stage it is unlikely assessments of the child's developmental level will be carried out.

If the problem is identified in the first few years, paediatricians are still likely to be the main professionals involved in the assessment although the referral will have come through the GP and health visitor. The paediatricians will also focus on questions about the name of the disability, causes and prognosis. However psychologists, either educational or clinical, and speech and language therapists may conduct a cognitive, developmental and linguistic assessment. These professionals are likely to focus on questions about the extent of the disability in a range of areas and on implications for programme planning. Similarly physiotherapists, audiologists and ophthalmologists may assess the extent of physical and sensory disabilities to help answer questions about the nature, cause and severity of the problem and to advise on programme planning.

Whether the problem is identified at birth or in the first few years of life, all professionals involved will assess the extent to which the family has adjusted to the reality that their son or daughter has learning difficulties and the extent to which community and local voluntary organizations may be able to offer support. Many hospitals employ social workers who will take the lead in this aspect of the assessment.

When discussing the assessment of children with learning difficulties in the first years of life it is important to remember that services vary across the country. Many health authorities have child development centres based at a local hospital, staffed by paediatricians, psychologists, speech therapists and social workers. Such centres can also call on the services of physiotherapists, occupational therapists, audiologists, ophthalmologists and other medical staff who have relevant specialist expertise. Assessments can be carried out at one time with the key professionals being present. This facilitates full consultation and discussion between all professionals and parents. Unfortunately there are still some health authorities whose child development centres are staffed inadequately, and parents may have to take their children to a range of different professionals at different times and in different locations. This can make assessments extremely time-consuming and frustrating for parents as, at each stage, they only receive partial answers to questions about their child's development. Furthermore the fact that professionals work in different settings makes it more difficult for them to consult with all those involved.

Assessment for educational provision (statementing procedures)

Under the 1993 Education Act it is the responsibility of the LEA to assess and make provision for pupils with special educational needs. This Act has introduced several major changes to its predecessor, the 1981 Education Act, which are designed to improve the delivery of services to these pupils and their families. These include the publication of the Code of Practice (DFE, 1994a) which strengthens procedures for school-based stages of assessment, suggests an enhanced role for special education needs co-ordinators and offers guidance on the criteria to follow when deciding whether to proceed to a statutory assessment. In addition there is a time limit of six months for the completion of statements, the appeals procedures have been amended and there are changes to ways in which annual reviews of statements should be conducted. The DFE have provided a guide for parents on the implementation of the 1993 Act (DFE, 1994b).

As regards the statutory procedures for the initial assessment of pupils with learning difficulties, the 1993 Act is little different from its predecessor. Assessments of these pupils should be carried out by a multidisciplinary team including a doctor, teacher and psychologist, although other professionals should be consulted as necessary. Parents should be fully involved at all stages of the assessment process and should be invited to contribute to it and submit reports from other professionals whom they have engaged. The professionals involved and parents submit reports (advice) to the LEA specifying the needs of the pupil, and the LEA is responsible for making provision to meet those needs. The statement, together with all reports, is sent to the parents. These and other procedures for drawing up statements should be familiar to all those who have been involved with both the 1981 and 1993 Acts.

It is likely that all pupils with moderate and severe learning difficulties will have a statement and that, for pupils with SLD, this will have been drawn up before they are five years old. Given the nature of the disabilities faced by pupils with more severe learning difficulties, they will almost certainly have been identified by the health services and assessed by a range of professionals before the statementing process is initiated. Indeed Section 176 of the 1993 Act states that:

> District Health Authorities (DHAs) and National Health Service (NHS) Trusts must inform the parents and the appropriate LEA when they form the opinion that a child under the age of five may have special educational needs. They must also inform the parents if they believe that a particular voluntary organisation is likely to be able to give the parents advice or assistance in connection with any special educational needs that the child may have. (Taken from page 101 of the Code of Practice, DFE, 1994a.)

On receipt of this information LEAs should have agreed procedures for acting quickly. For example the Code of Practice suggests that a pre-school adviser or educational psychologist should consult with personnel from the health service or that, if the child attends a nursery school, the LEA should expect the broad principles of the stage based assessment procedures, outlined in the Code, to have been followed and that some form of systematic intervention should have been implemented over a period of time.

For pupils with severe learning difficulties, where the presence of a disability is rarely in question, health services are likely to have a great deal of detailed information about the child at the time of referral to the LEA. Furthermore those involved in the assessment may have known for some time what the nature of the educational provision is likely to be following the statutory assessment. Therefore the role of the professionals involved in drawing up the statement can be one of confirming existing information about the child and his/her needs.

It is not uncommon for some LEAs to accelerate the process by drawing up interim statements on pupils with learning difficulties. As the need for provision and intervention is often quite urgent and all those involved are aware of the provision which will ultimately be made, LEAs may use interim statements to enable the pupil to attend the provision for an assessment period during which time the formal statutory assessment can be completed.

As stated in Chapter 9, the vast majority of pupils with learning difficulties still attend a special school. However there are increasing moves to provide more integrated placements and the period when the pupil is undergoing a statutory assessment should provide an ideal opportunity for professionals to discuss the full range of educational placements which might be available. Frequently the parents may come to the assessment having been informed by the medical professionals, with whom they have had contact up to then, that their child will inevitably have to go to a special school. They may have been 'conditioned' into accepting this as the only alternative. Educational personnel, in particular educational psychologists, should use the assessment as an opportunity to explore the full range of possible educational placements with the parents. It may well be the case that placement in a special school will not be the best option at this stage in the child's life.

Assessments leading up to school-leaving age – transition plans

The progress of all pupils with statements is reviewed annually (see below). All annual reviews following a pupil's fourteenth birthday must incorporate a transition plan. This should include details of how the pupil's programme will prepare him/her for transition into adult life. The social services must be informed that the pupil may require services on leaving school, and other agencies, including the careers service and staff at colleges of further education, should be invited to contribute to these assessments. However it is rare for medical personnel to be involved at this stage.

The aims of these reviews is to consider the appropriateness of the educational programme. However, in view of the pupil's impending move into the adult world, questions about provision inevitably surface, often having been dormant since the pupil was placed in his/her current school. Most LEAs have special schools which cater for pupils with severe learning difficulties until they reach the age of 19, if they and their parents request this. Therefore questions concerning future provision may not arise until well after the pupil's fourteenth birthday. Many parents express a great deal of concern at this stage of their child's life. On the whole, provision for school-aged pupils with learning difficulties is far superior to that which is offered to adults. Frequently an assessment of a student with learning difficulties can indicate clearly the ideal level of provision which should be offered but only rarely is this available.

Transition plans provide a mechanism to ensure that all professionals, the parents and the student can focus on the appropriate educational programme which will enable him/her to make a smooth transition into adult life. However, given the limited quality of provision which is available to most adults with learning difficulties, there may be problems in ensuring that these plans are fully implemented when the student leaves school.

This section has provided an overview of the contexts in which the assessments of pupils with learning difficulties may be carried out and the professionals who may be involved. There are also five further aspects of the assessment process which should also be considered.

First, periods when assessments may be conducted, highlighted above, should not be taken to imply that there are no other times when assessment takes place. As stated at the start of this chapter, assessment is a complex process involving many activities and many people. As far as pupils with learning difficulties are concerned parents and teachers, who have regular contact with the pupil, carry out ongoing daily assessments of their pupil and respond accordingly. These could be assessments of, for example, the pupil's mood or the length of time he/she is taking to complete daily living tasks. Teachers and parents may share their observations through the home-school diary and this helps them to work together for the benefit of the pupil. These ongoing assessments provide evidence for the success or otherwise of previous interventions and they help in planning further educational programmes. In terms of helping the pupil to make progress they are probably more useful than the more formal assessments referred to above. This process of ongoing assessment is similar to curriculum-based assessment which we will consider in more detail later in the chapter.

Second, in addition to this ongoing process of assessment and evaluation, LEAs are required to review all statements annually. The aims of the review are to assess the pupil's progress towards meeting the objectives specified in the statement and/or the previous annual review, to review the appropriateness of the provision and to consider whether the statements should be amended.

Headteachers are responsible for managing the review and for submitting a report to the LEA. They must seek written advice from the parents and invite them to a review meeting. Other professionals may also submit reports and/or be invited to the review. In practice the review always includes the headteacher or a representative, the class teacher and the parent. The involvement of other professionals is more varied and may include a speech and language therapist, a physiotherapist, an educational psychologist or a social worker. Paediatricians and other medical consultants rarely attend annual reviews.

As far as pupils with learning difficulties are concerned the annual review tends to focus on questions about the pupil's individual educational programme: is it relevant to meeting long-term needs, are targets being achieved, should changes be made? Although the reviews form an essential component in the delivery of effective services, they may not be seen by the parents as being as crucial as assessments which are carried out at other times in the pupil's life since major decisions about changes in provision tend not to be made.

Third, in the introduction to this book we referred to the fact that many professionals can be involved in working with a pupil with learning difficulties and the family, particularly when he/she is being formally assessed. In view of the complex nature of these pupils' problems multidisciplinary involvement is to be welcomed for it would be unrealistic for one professional to possess all the relevant information needed to provide advice and support to a pupil and the family. However, for multidisciplinary work to be effective, all agencies need to work well together and to appreciate each other's expertise. Too often there have been examples where professionals have failed to communicate with each other and have given parents conflicting advice.

Fourth, recently there has been a growing interest in finding ways of involving pupils in the assessment of pupils with special educational needs. The Code of Practice makes reference to the importance of doing this. As Mittler (1996) states, 'people with learning disabilities are, probably more than any group, disadvantaged by the fact that others have always spoken for them'. Wherever possible therefore it is important to involve pupils with learning difficulties in the process of the assessment. For pupils with profound and multiple learning difficulties this may not be possible and to include such people in a case conference, for example, can be tokenistic. However there are many pupils with learning difficulties who may be able to offer a great deal to their assessment and should be offered help and support in putting their views forward.

Finally, the vital role that parents play in assessment cannot be over-stressed. At all stages parents should be involved as equal partners. They are the only member of an assessment team who will have detailed knowledge of their pupil, and as a result they can contribute the most information. They will also be inexorably involved in the outcomes of the assessment. Their views should therefore be considered at all times.

There are however factors inherent in the assessment process which can make it difficult for parents to play a full part. For example, assessments are almost always carried out away from the pupil's home, e.g. at a school, hospital or clinic. Parents may feel quite uncomfortable in such settings which may not be all that familiar to them. They may be in awe of well-dressed, articulate professionals and, in their dealings with such people in the past, they may have adopted an attitude of 'They know best; who am I to question them?' These attitudes may result in parents' views being ignored and as a result the needs of the pupil are not met. Marks *et al* (1995) have shown that in annual review meetings parents are frequently talked *at* by teachers and they are given few opportunities to engage in meaningful dialogue. In addition, the seating arrangements are not conducive to an expression of a mutual exchange of views between everybody involved.

As we discussed in the introduction to this book, despite the rhetoric about parental involvement, it seems that we still have a long way to go before parents are seen as, and actually feel that they are, equal partners in the assessment process. Carpenter (1996) provides a helpful discussion of the issues involved in developing and improving effective partnership with parents.

ASSESSING PUPILS WITH LEARNING DIFFICULTIES: WHAT QUESTIONS ARE BEING ASKED?

In view of the complex nature of assessment and of the problems faced by pupils with learning difficulties, there are a whole variety of questions which parents and others may be asking when a pupil with learning difficulties is being assessed. These questions are directly related to the aims of the assessment, to the context in which it takes place and to the assessment methods used. In this section we shall discuss these different questions and the reasons why they may be asked.

1. Is there a problem in the pupil's development?
For many disabilities the answer to this question may be clear from birth, e.g. for children with cerebral palsy and Down's Syndrome. However, this is a question that a health visitor or doctor may ask for those children whose problems only become evident in the first few years of life. Alternatively a parent may consult such a person about, for example, their child's apparent slowness in developing language. Indeed some parents have complained that their health visitor or doctor has denied the existence of a problem or suggested that the child will 'grow out of it' implying, at the same time, that the parent is fussing. This has resulted in parents becoming angry at the late diagnosis of their child's disability and the consequent delay in doing anything about it.

2. How severe is the problem?
This question is closely linked to the first one. Having decided that there is a problem, it is important to establish how severe it is in all areas of development, for example motor and self-help skills, language and communication. For children whose problem is diagnosed at birth, assessments which address this question may not take place until the pupil is a few months old.

3. Does the disability have a name?

There are many pupils with learning difficulties who suffer from an associated condition, for example Down's Syndrome, cerebral palsy, Prader-Willi Syndrome, Rett Syndrome, epilepsy, autism, etc. A key question in assessment is whether such a label can be attached to the pupil. This may well have implications for the answers to questions 4, 5, and 6 below. In addition, parents may be put in touch with support groups or charitable organizations for families with children similar to their own, for example the Down's Syndrome Association or the National Autistic Society, who will be able to offer them help and guidance.

There are however many pupils with learning difficulties who do not appear to suffer from a specific syndrome or for whom no diagnosis has been offered. Hogg *et al* (1990) report that 50 per cent of a sample of 544 parents could not attach a syndrome or condition to their pupil with learning difficulties. These authors consider this to be a worrying finding as parents are typically very keen to attach a label to their child's disability.

4. What are the causes?

The answer to question 3 can also provide the answer to questions about causation. It is now well known, for example, that most cases of Down's Syndrome are caused by the presence of an extra chromosome. However the causes of conditions such as Prader-Willi and Rett Syndrome are still unclear. Nevertheless it is known that the causes of these and other syndromes are not related to environmental factors such as faulty child-rearing or accidents during pregnancy. This knowledge can come as a huge relief to the family, particularly in developing countries where there are still many myths surrounding the causes of disability and where, as stated earlier, it is not unknown for the presence of a disabled child to be viewed as a curse on the whole family.

Knowing the cause of the disability can also lead to claims for compensation, for example in cases of disability caused by whooping cough vaccination, or through injury sustained at birth. In these cases, particularly where there may be some dispute about the precise cause, the whole aim of assessment seems to focus on this question.

5. Is there a cure?

A natural question which parents often ask is whether there is a cure for their child's disability. After all, most illnesses suffered by children – e.g. measles, appendicitis – can be cured. There may be a perception that doctors are expected to cure their patients and it can come as a tremendous shock when parents realize that they are faced with a child who will have a lifelong disability. The search for a cure can lead parents to take quite extreme and expensive measures involving intensive therapy and treatment – 'patterning' (Doman 1974) being the best-known example. Although these treatments provided parents with support and hope for the future, evaluations of their effectiveness in terms of the gains made by children are at best inconclusive and at the present time the approach is hardly used.

6. What are the future long-term prospects?
If there is no 'cure' for the child's disability a further relevant question concerns the long-term prospects. Will the child grow up to be independent of the family, be able to manage daily living activities such as shopping, cleaning, washing, public transport? Will he/she be able to get married and raise a family? Or will he/she be dependent on others for support throughout his or her life?

7. How are the family coming to terms with having a child with learning difficulties in the family?
This is a key question for all those involved in working with the child and family, including the family members themselves, and the answer will have an important bearing on the child's development and on the extent to which families and professionals can work together. Carpenter (1996) suggests that some parents never completely get over the shock of having a child with a disability

8. What are the implications for educational provision?
For assessments which are carried out in the first five years of life this is a further crucial question. Should the child go to a special school or unit? Could he/she cope in a mainstream school? What provision is currently available in the LEA and what is their policy towards integration?

9. What are the implications for programme planning?
This question relates to the detailed educational and therapeutic interventions which should be offered by the school, medical personnel and the family. For example how does the result of the assessment relate to the specific programme of physiotherapy which is needed? What does it tell us about how to teach the child to communicate? These questions are frequently asked on a daily basis and are part of the ongoing process of assessment and evaluation which forms the core of good educational practice. Parents tend to ask this question when answers to more fundamental questions about the severity and causes of the disability have been answered and when the child has been offered educational provision.

METHODS OF ASSESSING PUPILS WITH LEARNING DIFFICULTIES

So far in this chapter we have considered the contexts in which assessments may be carried out, the professionals who may be involved and the questions which may be asked in assessment. When addressing these questions professionals need to employ a whole range of assessment methods which could include interviews, e.g. a family and medical history, systematic observation, a physical examination, developmental assessment, psychological testing and many other approaches. For example global questions, such as what is the extent of the problem (question 2), what school should the pupil go to (question 8), what will happen when he/she leaves school (question 6), require a different form of assessment than that which is needed when assessing the pupil's progress on daily teaching programmes (question 9).

In this section we shall review some of the assessment methods which may be used by teachers, psychologists and speech and language therapists and indicate which of the questions discussed in the previous section they are addressing. It is beyond the scope of this book to consider methods used by paediatricians and other medical personnel.

We shall begin with a review of the relevance of IQ testing for pupils with learning difficulties. This is followed by a discussion of the assessment of play and the use of developmental charts and checklists. Finally we consider the place of curriculum-based assessment.

Is there a place for IQ tests in the assessment of pupils with learning difficulties?

A great many publications about pupils with learning difficulties, including this one, make reference to IQ as one method of defining this group of pupils. In the Introduction we referred to the World Health Organisation's definition of moderate mental retardation as IQ 50–70 and severe retardation as IQ up to 50 (WHO, 1968). Other definitions based on IQ were also mentioned. The common reference to IQ as a means of classification suggests that IQ tests might be a useful tool in the assessment of individual pupils who have learning difficulties. However, as the whole question of IQ testing is controversial, the issue merits some discussion.

An IQ score is a normative measure which compares an individual's performance on a range of cognitive tasks with that of his/her peers. IQ tests are standardized instruments since, as part of their development, they were administered to a representative sample of pupils across the age range for which the tests were intended to be used. In this way test constructors obtain information about average, above and below average scores obtained by the 'normal' population. Most IQ tests have a mean of 100 and a standard deviation (SD) of 15. Therefore a score of 70 is two SDs and a score of 55 is three SDs below the mean. IQ scores of 70 are found in 2 per cent and scores of 55 in only 0.1 per cent of the population.

The best-known IQ tests commonly used in the UK are the Wechsler Intelligence for Children – WISC (Wechsler, 1992); and the British Ability Scales – BAS (Elliot *et al*, 1983). These and other similar tests are administered on a one-to-one basis by a trained clinical or educational psychologist. There are standard procedures to follow and strict scoring procedures. For most pupils it takes about one hour to administer each test.

The WISC is divided into five verbal and five non-verbal (performance scales), although there are two supplementary scales which can also be used. The verbal scales include tests of verbal reasoning, vocabulary, general knowledge and short-term memory. The non-verbal scales contain visio-spatial tests, a test which involves arranging a series of pictures such that they tell a story, and a coding test. The BAS contains twenty-three scales and this allows the test user to be flexible in the choice of scales to use when assessing an individual pupil. This test is also divided into two parts, referred to as verbal and visual scales. Like the WISC the verbal scales contain measures of verbal reasoning, vocabulary, and short-term memory, and the visual scales contain measures of visio-spatial ability. However the BAS also contains measures of speed, non-verbal reasoning and basic literacy skills. Furthermore, unlike the WISC, some of the scales have been designed for pre-school pupils, for example the scales which measure verbal comprehension and naming vocabulary.

In general terms a full-scale IQ score (i.e. one that is derived for an assessment of the pupil's performance on all scales of the test appropriate for the age of the pupil) gives an indication of how far behind the norm a pupil is functioning on a variety of cognitive skills. Hence it provides an answer to question 2, above, about the severity of the problem. For example, as referred to above, a pupil with an IQ of 55 achieves a score which is found in only 0.1 per cent of the population. This indicates that he/she has severe difficulties in completing items on the IQ test which are thought to be related to general cognitive functioning and learning ability.

There are a number or fundamental objections to the use of full-scale IQ tests in the assessment of pupils with learning difficulties. Some of these are discussed by Mittler (1992), Berger and Yule, (1985,

1987), Hogg and Sebba (1986) and Selfe (1993). These objections can be summarized as follows.

1. An IQ test is administered on a one-to-one basis and testing follows a standard procedure. Many pupils with learning difficulties are unable to respond to this traditional 'testing' situation because of their physical and sensory difficulties, problems in language and communication and in their ability to concentrate. These difficulties may make it impossible to administer several scales of an IQ test and the reliability of the scores obtained on those that are administered may be in serious doubt. These difficulties are even more apparent when administering a traditional IQ test to pupils with PMLD – indeed it is simply not possible to begin to administer an IQ test to such pupils.
2. In view of the difficulties in administering tests to pupils with learning difficulties, tests such as the WISC and the BAS were not standardized on this population. This means that many pupils with learning difficulties either do not register a score on many scales, or they complete scales which have not been standardized on pupils of their age.
3. An IQ score tells us nothing about a pupil's performance on basic skills related to the curriculum. It therefore offers no suggestions for individual programme planning.
4. Contrary to earlier beliefs about IQ scores being fixed measures of potential, it is now well known that they can change dramatically and therefore placements in special schools based on these measures can be extremely inappropriate and not in the best interests of the pupil.

These concerns about the use of full-scale IQ tests in the assessment of individual pupils with learning difficulties mean that such tests are rarely used. In a small-scale survey Jones (1991) interviewed thirty clinical and educational psychologists about the procedures they used to assess pre-school pupils with language and learning difficulties. Only one psychologist regularly used the BAS and three sometimes used it. Two others regularly used the Stanford Binet Test and one sometimes used the Wechsler Pre-School and Primary Scale of Intelligence (WPPSI), a related test to the WISC, but used with young pupils.

Although full-scale IQ tests are rarely used when assessing pupils with learning difficulties, there are occasions when it might be appropriate to use parts of an IQ test, or more specialist tests of cognitive function in order to evaluate a pupil's ability on a particular aspect of development. It is possible, for example, to use the Verbal Comprehension and Naming Vocabulary scales of the BAS for pupils with learning difficulties. Both scales are clearly relevant to pupils' linguistic development and the resulting scores do give an indication of how severe the problem is in this area. Similarly the British Picture Vocabulary Scale (Dunn *et al*, 1982) provides a measure of receptive vocabulary. Finally the non-verbal items of the Merrill Palmer Scale (Stutsman, 1931), although extremely dated, remain very attractive to pupils and therefore some useful information about a pupil's ability to complete puzzles and similar items can be obtained from this test. However as it is such a long time since it was standardized, the resulting scores should be treated with extreme caution. All the above measures provide answers to question 2 above about the severity of a pupil's problems in cognitive areas.

The assessment of play

Carefully structured observation of the level of play of a pupil with learning difficulties provides an important and effective alternative to the formal assessment of pupils using traditional tests. Authors such as Lowe and Costello (1976), McConkey and Jeffree (1979, 1980) and Newson (1993) have stressed the relevance of the assessment of play for these pupils.

Newson (*op. cit.*), for example, provides guidelines on the specific areas of a child's development on which the assessment of play should focus. These are summarized below.

1. *The general social impression.* For example does the pupil co-operate with others, does he/she make eye contact, is he/she 'comfortable' with the person carrying out the observation, does he/she respond if demands are made or does a temper tantrum usually follow?
2. *The pupil's ability to imitate.* Does the pupil imitate a person's sounds or actions? This behaviour indicates that he/she is aware of the presence of that person and usually means that he/she can take part in 'imitation games'. Imitation is an important prerequisite for learning to sign and to make speech sounds.
3. *The pupil's ability to follow instructions.* In particular it is important to see if verbal instructions, given without gesture, can be followed or whether the pupil only focuses on gesture. Sometimes the understanding of instructions is dependent on them being given in a familiar situation or by a particular person.
4. *Reciprocal play.* Can the pupil interact with another person in a play situation? For example can he/she roll a ball back to someone who has rolled it to them? Does the pupil understand about turn taking?

5. *Speech and communication.* How does the pupil indicate his or her needs? Is language used or if not, are gesture or mime used?
6. *Problem-solving: Strategies and skills.* How does the pupil solve 'straightforward' problems such as how to get a toy from a shelf or more complex ones involved in completing a puzzle? Are trial and error strategies used or does the pupil appear to be thinking the problem through?
7. *Symbolic play (pretending).* Does the pupil show evidence of pretending while playing, i.e. taking on a role when playing with toys? For example does he/she use a different voice when handling a doll as if the child is trying to act as a mum or dad? Assessing symbolic play is dealt with in more detail later in this section.
8. *Hand-eye and whole-body co-ordination.* Observing a pupil at play provides an excellent opportunity to observe the pupil's overall co-ordination, where there are problems, the type of tasks he/she is good at.

Newson provides comprehensive advice about the range of toys which will facilitate accurate observation and she also stresses that observational assessment is not a once and for all activity. Teachers and parents need to observe pupils continually as part of ongoing assessment. Indeed Newson considers that findings from assessing a pupil's level of play can be directly linked to programme planning, i.e. they help to provide answers to question 9 above.

Lowe and Costello (1976) developed a 'test' of symbolic play which provides normative information about a pupil's development in this area. The aim of the test is to assess 'the pupil's ability to appreciate semantic rather than spatial relationships, his early concepts, and his ability to deal with symbols in their simplest form' (p. 5). Although referred to as a 'test' it is administered quite informally. The pupil is observed playing with objects which should be familiar to him/her – for example, a doll, brush, cup and spoon; or a tractor and trailer – and his/her behaviour is recorded. High scores are obtained if pupils play imaginatively with all of the toys. Essentially this is a normative test as it provides data about the level of play which a pupil has reached. It therefore answers questions about how far behind a pupil might be in this area of development – question 2 above.

A more extensive development of this work has been carried out by McConkey and Jeffree (1979, 1980). They identified five different stages in the development of pretend play and suggested that, through careful observation of the child playing with a range of toys, it is possible to assess which stage of play the pupil usually engages in. The five stages are:

1. *Exploratory play:* mouthing objects, looking at them, throwing or banging them;
2. *Relational play:* putting objects in containers, putting them on top of each other;
3. *Self-pretending:* feeding self with spoon, brushing one's own hair;
4. *Decentred pretending:* feeding a doll or another person;
5. *Sequence pretending:* linking pretend actions together, feeding a doll, self or adult; undressing a doll, putting it in the bath, turning on the taps, washing it.

In the first two stages the pupil does not distinguish between the objects. All of them may be mouthed or thrown, put in a box or taken out again. Only in stage 3 does the pupil start to discriminate between the objects, e.g. spoons are for feeding, brushes are for brushing one's hair. However, pretending doesn't really begin until stage 4 when the pupil 'pretends' to feed a doll or another person. This is extended in stage 5 when the pupil starts to play imaginary games, such as putting a doll to bed, which involve a complex sequence of pretend actions. In any one play session a pupil will oscillate from one stage of play to another and it is only after a number of observations that one can gain an accurate picture of the stages of play that the pupil typically engages in. This provides helpful information for teachers and parents as to the next stages of play which should be developed – answering question 9, above, on the implications of assessment for programme planning.

One of the key aims in the assessment of play, referred to by all the above authors, is to gain information about the pupil's ability to think and to play imaginatively. This is done through observing the way pupils play with toys while not requiring them to use language. The findings can provide a clue as to the extent to which they may be able to learn to communicate. Hence the assessment of play may begin to provide answers to question 6 above concerning the long-term prospects for the pupil. For if pupils cannot communicate verbally and they show no evidence of imaginative play and symbolic thinking, then the overall outlook for the development of language and communication skills is not very good.

Developmental charts and checklists

Developmental charts and checklists are perhaps the tools most commonly used by psychologists, paediatricians, teachers, speech therapists and others in the assessment of pupils with learning difficulties, especially severe learning difficulties. In particular they are used to answer questions about how far behind a pupil is and what school he/she should attend (questions 2 and 8 above). However, as we shall see, some developmental charts and checklists also address questions about programme planning (question 9).

Developmental charts contain a number of items (behaviours which pupils learn) arranged in the order in which they are normally acquired. These items on the charts are usually divided into different areas of development. Typically these include the following:

- language development (receptive and expressive);
- self-help skills (e.g. feeding, dressing, personal hygiene);
- physical development (fine and gross motor skills).

However there is considerable variation between different charts in the areas they include. Many charts are norm referenced, in that the age when most pupils would be expected to achieve each item, or group of items, is included. Therefore it is possible to see at a glance, once the assessment is completed, how far behind a pupil is from other pupils of his or her age. However, the results are not particularly helpful as a basis for planning intervention programmes. Those charts which contain many items in each area (e.g. the Portage Checklist – see below) can be used for programme planning purposes. Norm referenced charts contain items up to a developmental age of between 5 and 6 years. These norms have been derived from books on child development, and/or they may have been taken from standardized tests which include similar items. Developmental charts, therefore, are not standardized instruments in the same way the IQ tests are standardized. Some charts contain no information about the age at which normally developing children might achieve each item. These tend to be quite detailed and may only focus on one aspect of development, for example the Assessment of Early Feeding and Drinking Skills (Coupe *et al*, 1987) or the Pathways to Independence (PATH) Checklist (Jeffree and Cheseldine, 1982), a checklist of skills needed for independent living.

A developmental chart is usually completed by a psychologist or other professional who goes through the items on the chart with the parents and asks them whether the child can 'do' the items on a regular basis. Often the parents may be unsure whether the pupil can do (or pass) an item and so it will be necessary to observe the pupil trying to complete the specific task referred to on an item. Many charts can be completed in one session. However, the more able the pupil and the more detailed the chart, the longer it takes to complete and several sessions will be needed. Sometimes a teacher will be asked to complete a developmental chart as well as the parents.

There are several developmental charts and checklists which are commonly used in the UK and the USA. In this chapter there is only space to refer to the two most commonly referred-to charts in the Jones' (1991) survey of assessment methods used by psychologists. There were the Parental Involvement Project (PIP) charts and the Portage Checklist.

The PIP charts (Jeffree and McConkey, 1976) arose out of a parent involvement project in which the authors were involved. Essentially they are norm referenced (0–5 years) and cover the following areas of development: physical development, social development, eye-hand development, the development of play and language development. Figure 2.1 shows part of the charts taken from the Self-Help area.

Section 5: Toileting

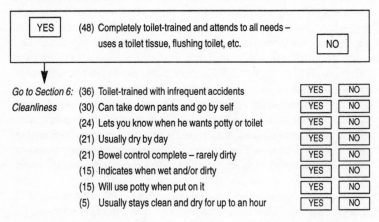

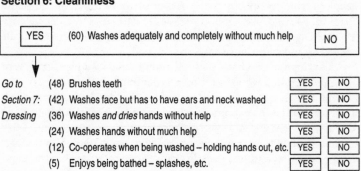

Go to Section 7: Dressing

Figure 2.1   Part of the Self-Help area taken from the PIP Developmental Charts

An unusual feature of the PIP charts concerns the first item on each section – the one in the box (see Figure 2.1). If a pupil can do this item, one should proceed to the next section. If the pupil cannot do the item, the parents are asked to go through the other items within the section. This procedure enables one to move through the chart quite quickly. The numbers in brackets refer to the age in months at which most children would be expected to be able to do an item.

The Portage Checklist (White and Cameron, 1987) was originally developed in the USA as part of the Portage Project and is used extensively in many countries. The checklist is divided into the following areas: socialization, self-help, cognitive, motor, language, infant stimulation. It is norm referenced (0–6 years) except for the infant stimulation scale which is only used for pupils with PMLD. However, the items are grouped into age bands and therefore it is not possible to state the age at which pupils should be able to do each individual item. There are many more items on the Portage Checklist when compared with the PIP charts. This means that it takes longer to complete, up to four visits, according to many Portage home visitors. However, the information gained is far more detailed than it is on PIP. As a result the Portage Checklist can be used for programme planning. Indeed the Portage kit includes a set of activity cards linked to every item on the chart. These cards provide suggestions as to how each item may be taught. Thus the Portage Checklist can be seen as a whole curriculum. Figure 2.2 provides a sample of items from the motor area of the Portage chart.

If a pupil is beginning to achieve an item, White and Cameron (1987) suggest that a tick is placed just outside and to the left of the column headed 'Entry behaviour'. If the pupil can 'perform the skill correctly and on request' the tick is placed inside this column. The 'Date achieved' column can be used to record the date at which a pupil achieved the skill and the 'Comments' can be used to make a note on the pupil's performance. White and Cameron (*op. cit.*) provide detailed guidance on how to introduce and complete the checklist. They also suggest that the pupil should be asked to complete each item rather than solely relying on information from the parents.

The following is a list of the advantages of using developmental charts as part of the assessment of pupils with learning difficulties.

- They provide information about how far behind a pupil is in each of the areas covered on the chart.
- They can be used to plan intervention programmes, particularly those charts containing many items.
- They can be used to help make decisions about educational provision.

Portage Checklist

© CESA 5 and NFER-NELSON

Age levels 0–1 (1–45); 1–2 (46–63); 2–3 (64–80); 3–4 (81–95); 4–5 (96–111); 5–6 (112–140)

Card Behaviour		Entry Behaviour	Date Achieved	Comments
1	Reaches for object 15–22cm in front of him			
2	Grasps object held 8cm in front of him			
3	Reaches and grasps object in front of him			
4	Reaches for preferred object			
5	Puts object in mouth			
6	Head and chest supported on arms while on stomach			
7	Holds head and chest erect supported on one arm			
8	Feels and explores object with mouth			
9	Turns from stomach to side, maintains position 50% of time			
10	Rolls from stomach to back			
11	Moves forward one body length on stomach			
12	Rolls from back to side			
13	Turns from back to stomach			
14	Pulls to sitting position when grasping adult's fingers			
15	Turns head freely when body is supported			
16	Maintains sitting position for 2 minutes			
17	Puts down one object deliberately to reach for another			
18	Picks up and drops object on purpose			
19	Stands with maximum support			
20	Bounces up and down in standing position while being supported			
21	Crawls one body length to obtain object			
22	Sits self-supported			
23	From sitting position, turns to hands and knees position			
24	Moves from stomach to sitting position			
25	Sits without hand support			
26	Flings objects haphazardly			
27	Rocks back and forth on hands and knees			
28	Transfers objects from one hand to the other in sitting position			
29	Retains 2cm cubes in one hand			
30	Pulls self to on-knees position			
31	Pulls self to standing position			
32	Uses pincer grasp to pick up object			
33	Crawls on hands and knees			
34	Reaches with one hand from crawling position			
35	Stands with minimum support			
36	Licks food from around mouth			
37	Stands alone for 1 minute			
38	Tips out object from receptacle			
39	Turns pages of book, several at a time			
40	Scoops with spoon or shovel			
41	Puts small objects in container			
42	Lowers self from standing to sitting position			
43	Claps hands			

Figure 2.2 Part of the Motor section of the Portage Checklist

- They can be administered flexibly with the full involvement of parents.
- They do not have to be completed in one session.
- If a parent and teacher completes a chart on the same pupil, the results can be used to compare each person's perception of the pupil. This helps to add validity to the findings and also highlights areas where there may be disagreements.
- If they are administered again after a period of time, e.g. six months or a year, the results can be used to assess a pupil's progress over that period.

There are, however, some problems to be aware of in the administration and interpretation of developmental charts. First, many pupils with more severe learning difficulties will, by definition, be developing extremely slowly and a developmental chart will illustrate this problem only too clearly. As this may be the first time that every aspect of a child's development is being assessed in such detail, it may be hard for the parents to assimilate the information. Although parents are usually well aware of their children's problems, to see on a chart, for example, that their pupil is only functioning at the six-month level when he/she is 5 years old adds clarity to the problem which is not always easy to take in and may cause some distress. Developmental charts therefore have to be administered sensitively with the emphasis being on what the pupil can achieve rather than on what he/she is unable to do.

Second, some items on a chart are extremely fuzzy and it may be difficult to determine whether or not the pupil can 'do' the item. For example what exactly does the item 'usually dry by day' (from the P.I.P. Chart above) actually mean? In particular, how does one define 'usually'? Third, the lack of standardization means that the norms may be inaccurate. For this reason age levels should always be quoted as approximations and treated with extreme caution.

Despite some of the problems with developmental charts they remain a key tool in the assessment of pupils with learning difficulties. They are most likely to be used immediately prior to the introduction of a pre-school home visiting service such as Portage or prior to the pupil starting school. The information will help parents and teachers to obtain a picture of how far behind the norm a pupil is in important areas of development and it may also be used in programme planning. Developmental charts can also be used prior to annual reviews or when the pupil is about to leave school. However, at both these stages curriculum-based assessment may be just as appropriate.

Curriculum-based assessment

Essentially curriculum-based assessment (CBA) is something which teachers have been engaged in for years and it is not a technique which is restricted to the assessment of pupils with special needs. Essentially CBA involves the assessment of the progress each pupil is making on the curriculum and is directly related to question 9 above. To do this successfully it is necessary for each school to have a carefully planned curriculum with accompanying record sheets which enable the pupil's progress to be recorded clearly and without taking up too much time. This information can be used to evaluate the success of each individual programme and to plan new ones. Therefore in CBA, assessment and intervention go hand in hand. As stated above the results of CBA can also be used in annual reviews and when the pupil is coming up to leaving school.

This form of assessment is similar to continuous formative assessment discussed by Lewis (1996). She summarizes some of the key questions about assessment that schools should consider which are taken from the NFER report (NFER, 1995; Fletcher-Campbell, 1996; and from SCAA, 1996). These are as follows:

- Is assessment sufficiently accurate and focused to inform future teaching and to enable the setting of goals?
- Are assessment opportunities and activities built into schemes of work/programmes of learning?
- Do records include details of pupils' experiences or achievements and, if appropriate, the extent of support provided?
- Is assessment used to monitor progression towards short- and long-term goals?
- Is assessment used as a way of recognizing and valuing all achievements and progress, however small, in all aspects of the curriculum and in whatever contexts?
- Is pupils' participation in self-assessment and recording actively promoted?
- What evidence is kept and collated to support teachers' assessments?

(Taken from Lewis, 1996)

Lewis (*op. cit.*) also provides guidance as to how teachers can carry out detailed assessments through general classroom and systematic observation and by working individually with pupils. Her chapter reflects the fact that accurate curriculum-based assessment, review and evaluation are an essential part of effective teaching and learning.

SUMMARY

Throughout this chapter we have referred to the range of different questions which may be asked when a pupil with learning difficulties is being assessed, to the occasions (contexts) when they might be asked, the people who could be involved in answering them and the techniques that might be used. In discussing these techniques we have restricted ourselves to a review of the use of intelligence tests, observation methods to assess play, developmental charts and checklists and to curriculum-based assessment. These assessments will normally be carried out by psychologists, teachers, speech therapists and paediatricians. Other techniques, involving medical and neurological examinations and taking a family history, have not been considered. However they also have an important part to play in the whole assessment process.

A summary of the questions being asked in assessment, the professionals involved and the techniques that might be used is provided in Table 2.1. This table encapsulates the whole chapter and, in so doing, places assessment within a coherent framework.

Clearly there is a risk that the broad overview provided in Table 2.1 masks the complexity of the assessment process. Therefore it is important to supplement the table with the following concluding comments:

1. The table makes no reference to parents. As referred to earlier in the chapter, they are integral to the assessment process and may well be one of the key people asking and answering the questions. It goes without saying that parents must be fully involved throughout the assessment. They also can help in completing developmental charts and in carrying out careful observations of their children.
2. It is important to recognize that different people will be asking different questions and that, almost certainly, they will only have the expertise to answer some of them. They will therefore use completely different assessment techniques. For example, a paediatrician may be looking for a diagnosis, i.e. answering questions 3 and 4 concerning the name and causes of the disability. To answer these questions he/she will probably carry out medical and neurological examinations, techniques which other professionals are not trained to use. A teacher and a psychologist may employ a developmental assessment to find out how far behind other pupils the child is, i.e. answering question 2, using techniques that are probably unfamiliar to medical personnel. There are also some techniques (e.g. interviewing families, gaining rapport with

Questions	Age when questions may be asked	Professionals involved in answering the questions	Assessment methods used
1. Is there a problem?	At birth or up to 5 years	Paediatricians, GP, health visitors, speech therapists, psychologists	Medical examination, developmental chart, observation, psychometric tests
2. How severe is the problem?	As above + on leaving school	As above + nursery school teacher, home visitor	As above
3. Does the disability have a name?	At birth or up to 5 years	Paediatricians, speech therapist, psychologist	Medical examination, observation
4. What are the causes?	As above	As above	Medical examination, 'history' of the disability
5. Is there a cure?	As above	As above	As above
6. What are the long-term prospects?	As above + on leaving school	As above + nursery teacher, home visitor	Medical examination, observation, developmental chart, psychometric test
7. How are the family coming to terms with the disability?	At all times in child's life	As above + social workers	Family interview/observation
8. What are the implications for provision?	At birth or up to 5 years or on leaving school	Psychologist, speech therapist, physiotherapist, teachers of visually and hearing impaired pupils, home visitors, teachers	Developmental chart, observation, psychometric test, CBA, visual and audiological assessment
9. What are the implications for programme planning?	At all times in pupil's life	As above	CBA, some developmental charts, observation, visual and audiological assessment

Table 2.1: The assessment of pupils with learning difficulties: an overview

pupils), which may be common to all professionals. If all those involved are aware of the range of questions which are being asked and about each person's role in answering them, the assessment should proceed smoothly. Indeed this is the hallmark of effective multidisciplinary assessment.

3. There can be times, however, when someone is carrying out an assessment to answer one particular question which other parties to the assessment are not even asking. For example a teacher may be involved in carrying out a detailed curriculum-based assessment prior to a meeting with the parent in order to answer questions about the pupil's individual programme. However, the parents may still have unanswered questions about the causes of the disability or whether it has a name. As no answers to these important questions have been provided to their satisfaction, they may find it hard to focus on questions concerning programme planning and may therefore feel unable to co-operate with the teacher in running a programme. Teachers need to be sensitive to parents' feelings on such issues and not dismiss them as being unco-operative just because they do not work collaboratively with the school.

4. Finally it is important to draw attention to one aspect of the assessment of pupils with learning difficulties which has not so far been referred to, that is the assessment of settings and the people in them, for example, the agencies available to help the pupil, the schools and the community. Pupils do not live in a vacuum and when answering questions 8 and 9 in particular, it is important to be aware of the settings where pupils may be placed. All professionals assess settings as part of their work. For example we continually make judgements about what is a 'good' school or service. Whether the methods we use to make these judgements are accurate, appropriate or understood is an open question. Frequently these judgements may be based on an unfortunate first impression or on what another professional has said following a visit to an establishment which was made many years ago. Whether professionals can act on these assessments in an honest way is also an area of concern. For example, suppose that an educational psychologist (EP) has carried out an assessment and considers that a pupil has a profile of needs which would require a particular type of school or service. If the only school which could meet the pupil's needs within the LEA is thought to be inadequate, does the EP inform the parent? This is a very real dilemma for EPs, as informing the parent may delay the whole process of providing appropriate education for the pupil, it may result in the parents making representations to the LEA and the EP will get into trouble

with his/her superior officers and with the staff in the school in question. To avoid these problems it is not uncommon for EPs to keep quiet about their views on the recommended school and hope that it will improve and that the pupil will derive sufficient benefit from the placement for it to meet his/her needs.

Professionals working in a multidisciplinary context also assess each other – and again this assessment is done informally and is not reported other than in 'gossip' between professionals who know each other well. These 'assessments' can dramatically affect the course of an assessment of a pupil with learning difficulties. If, for example, a teacher doubts the competence of a professional colleague in another discipline, he/she may try to refer a pupil to someone else. If this is not successful and the pupil has to see this 'incompetent' professional, the teacher may 'prime' the parents beforehand in order to ensure that the assessment proceeds as smoothly as possible. However, such actions may get the teacher into trouble and therefore he/she may behave in the same way as the EP and say nothing in the hope that everything will turn out satisfactorily.

CHAPTER 3

Behavioural teaching methods: overview and critique

INTRODUCTION

Without doubt theories derived from behavioural psychology have had a major impact on professional practice in the field of learning difficulties over the last thirty years. Indeed in the 1980s the vast majority of publications on teaching pupils with learning difficulties stressed the importance of the behavioural approach. The Skills Analysis Model (Gardner *et al*, 1983), the Portage Project (White and Cameron, 1987), EDY (Foxen and McBrien, 1981) the SNAP materials (Ainscow and Muncey, 1984), ELSA (Ainscow and Tweddle, 1984), Precision Teaching (Raybould and Solity, 1988 a and b) are some examples. These and other materials reflected a level of expertise in the application of behavioural methods which had not been seen before. For pupils with severe learning difficulties, Portage continues to flourish not only in the UK but throughout the world and EDY, now revised and updated (McBrien *et al*, 1992; Farrell *et al*, 1992), continues to be popular. Indeed EDY has recently been adapted for used in India (Farrell and Banerjee, 1996).

Although behavioural teaching methods have been extremely influential, in the past few years there has been an increasing number of publications which have criticized, either directly or by implication, the use of this approach (see, for example, Billinge, 1988; Emblem and Conti-Ramsden, 1991; Tilstone, 1991; Sebba *et al*, 1995; Glenn and O'Brien, 1994; Byers, 1994). Furthermore, books by authors previously committed to the approach (for example Ainscow and Tweddle, 1988; Ainscow and Muncey, 1989) are less overtly behavioural in orientation. The broadly based teaching methodologies suggested by the National Curriculum Development Team (learning difficulties) at the University of Cambridge, reflected in the *NCC Curriculum Guidance No. 9, Pupils with Severe Learning Difficulties*, NCC (1992) and later by Sebba *et al* (1995), is further evidence of this trend.

As stated in the Preface, one of the aims of this volume is to describe and evaluate the application of effective teaching strategies for pupils with learning difficulties (Chapters 4 and 5, in particular, focus on this area). Since many of these strategies are derived from behavioural psychology, it is important to consider some of the arguments about their effectiveness, particularly in view of recent concerns expressed by the authors referred to above. Therefore this chapter begins with a brief review of the key principles underpinning the behavioural approach and this is followed by a discussion of some of the major criticisms.

WHAT IS BEHAVIOURAL TEACHING?

Behavioural teaching, behavioural methods, the behavioural approach, are terms which are used interchangeably and in this chapter relate exclusively to teaching pupils with learning difficulties. Details of how behavioural methods can be used to teach pupils with learning difficulties are provided in Chapters 4 and 5. There is also an extensive literature on the subject (see, for example, Martin and Pear, 1988; Remington, 1991; Carr and Collins, 1992). In this chapter, therefore, we shall not examine all aspects of the behavioural approach in great detail. Instead, in order to set the scene for the discussion which follows, we shall review some of the following key inter-related aspects of the approach.

1. The behavioural approach takes as its starting point the premise that behaviour does not occur in isolation, that there are setting conditions, antecedents and consequences which influence the way we all behave. By carefully studying the nature of any or all of these, it is possible to plan behavioural change in a systematic way which is rewarding for everybody involved. We can all think of times when our work has been affected by the noise level around us (setting condition), by the task being too difficult (antecedent), or by the lack of feedback (consequences). Reflecting on these three factors should help us and our colleagues to improve the situation.
2. There are some key behavioural teaching techniques such as prompting, modelling, fading, shaping and reinforcement which, when used sensitively and appropriately, can help all people learn new tasks, either in one-to-one teaching or in group work.
3. When deciding on a teaching programme, it is important to set clear and unambiguous objectives so that everybody knows what the pupil should be doing when he/she has completed the programme. Related to this is the need to assess accurately the pupil's

current level of competence and to break tasks down into manageable steps. This is the key to planning any individual learning programme and is reflected in the guidance provided by the government on the implementation of the Code of Practice on the Identification and Assessment of Special Educational Needs (DFE, 1994).

In the past, many special schools, aided by books by Ainscow and Tweddle (1979, 1984) and Gardner *et al* (1983), have extended this idea and developed objectives-based curricula. Indeed, perhaps the 'objectives' approach to individual programme planning and curriculum development has been regarded as the cornerstone of behavioural teaching, providing as it does a systematic way of planning teaching programmes for pupils in a whole range of curriculum areas which can be carefully monitored and evaluated.

This extremely brief review of the behavioural approach to teaching pupils with learning difficulties is only meant to act as a reminder about its key principles. In addition to the standard texts which explain the application of behavioural psychology in more detail, there is a whole range of training packages designed to help people to use the approach including EDY and Portage. However, behavioural methods are relevant to the way we all learn and behave and are not restricted to people who have learning difficulties. One way of illustrating this point is to consider how a driving instructor plans to teach a new recruit to learn to drive a car. When planning and teaching this task the instructor will:

1. ask about the learner's previous experience of driving (Baseline);
2. know the standard of driving that the learner should reach before being entered for a driving test (Behavioural Objective);
3. know the component sub-skills that make up the skill of learning to drive and the order in which they are usually taught (Task Analysis);
4. adapt the teaching sequence if the learner progresses more quickly or more slowly than expected (Revise the Task Analysis);
5. demonstrate how to perform certain parts of the skill (Modelling);
6. help the learner to master different steps (Prompting);
7. inform the learner when he/she is making progress (Reinforcement);
8. be aware of the possible effect on the learner's progress of the traffic conditions, the weather, road works, etc. (Taking account of the Setting Conditions);
9. encourage the learner to practise driving another vehicle between lessons (Generalization).

In this example, adapted from McBrien *et al* (1992), the driving instructor is using behavioural teaching methods described in more detail in the following two chapters. Hence these methods can be applied to all of us. The majority of teachers, parents (and driving instructors) do not require specific training in the application of these techniques as most people do not experience great difficulties in learning. However, in order to teach pupils with learning difficulties, it is important for teachers to be aware of, and preferably be trained in, ways of applying behavioural methods successfully in their daily work.

SOME CONCERNS ABOUT STRUCTURED BEHAVIOURAL TEACHING METHODS

As mentioned in the introduction to this chapter, behavioural methods have been extremely influential although, in recent years, a number of concerns about the approach have been raised. In the remainder of this chapter we shall consider these concerns in some detail.

Objectives-based curricula are not suitable for all areas of the curriculum.
This criticism reflects something of a misunderstanding about behavioural teaching. These curricula were never intended to cover all areas of learning. Nor were pupils expected to work through tightly structured objectives-based teaching programmes all day. Ainscow and Tweddle (1979), for example, referred to the 'open' and 'closed' curriculum; the closed 'objectives'-based curriculum being used for approximately half the day and the open 'experiential' curriculum being applied at other times.

However, the objectives approach can be successfully applied to teach many new skills, particularly at the acquisition stage of learning (Haring *et al*, 1981; see also Chapter 5). In particular, it is useful for teaching key areas of the curriculum such as self help tasks, gross and fine motor skills, early number and reading, object recognition, object naming and signing. Indeed, objectives-based curricula have tended to focus on these areas.

This approach to curriculum and programme planning is less appropriate when the aim is to teach pupils to express new and creative ideas 'from within' and not to have to follow a predetermined path, as is the case in a behavioural programme. One would not, for example, use structured behavioural objectives to teach a group of nursery-age pupils to play together in the 'home' corner. Similarly, one would not use this method to teach an adolescent with learning difficulties to tell you what he/she felt about the television pro-grammes that were seen the night before. Interactive approaches (see below) may be more appropriate in these areas, particularly if behavioural techniques such as rewarding, prompting and shaping are built into the teaching.

Some objectives curricula have attempted to break down the teaching of language into a hierarchically ordered sequence of steps and it is perhaps in this area where the approach has most problems, as language programmes derived from these curricula are frequently sterile, overly structured and unrelated to the context in which the language will be used. See Harris (1988) for an excellent analysis of the issues involved.

It is helpful at this point to refer to the *National Curriculum Council Guidance No. 9* (NCC 1992). This booklet is primarily aimed at staff who work with SLD but the principles contained in it could equally be applied to all pupils with learning difficulties. The booklet stresses the need to extend and build on curriculum development work that has always been a feature in SLD schools. Some curriculum areas need to be defined as precisely as possible (as in an objectives-based curriculum) with 'predetermined performance criteria'. Others do not require this level of specificity. The overall balance depends on, among other things, the assessed needs and wishes of the pupil. This philosophy is further expanded by Sebba *et al* (1995).

It is possible, as Byers (1994) asserts, that in the enthusiasm to adopt a behaviourally orientated objectives-based curriculum, teaching programmes became too narrow and segmented within each individual curriculum area even though they were never intended to be applied in this way. Publications emanating from Sebba and her colleagues at Cambridge and the recent book edited by Carpenter *et al* (1996), have redressed the balance.

Behavioural methods deny the pupil the chance to take an active part in choosing what should be taught.
The implication is that in behavioural teaching, pupils are passive recipients of what others decide they should learn. Hence, their right to take an active part in choosing what they should learn is denied to them and this can result in tasks being taught which are of no value and which hold no intrinsic interest. Tilstone (1991), for example, implies that the behavioural approach can misuse and possibly exploit the power relationship between teacher and student. She argues that teachers should become facilitators, empowerers, consultants and partners, rather than directors and instructors in the learning process.

This criticism reflects a misunderstanding of the behavioural approach for two reasons. First, there is no reason why the pupil cannot be fully consulted about what he/she should be taught whatever approach is being used, including a behavioural one. Indeed, it is good practice to do this wherever possible and, as Mittler (1996b) reminds us, helping pupils with learning difficulties to make choices is one of the cornerstones of self-advocacy. If the pupil is keen to learn something and chooses the activity, then there is a much greater chance that the programme will be a success. If the pupil does not have the ability to express a preference verbally, through careful observation it should be possible to select teaching tasks in which he/she is interested.

Second, the sensitive teacher using behavioural techniques will, wherever possible, ask the pupil to discuss the teaching method to use, the settings where teaching will take place, the most appropriate task analysis and so on. Even for pupils with profound and multiple learning difficulties it is possible, through careful observation, to detect which aspects of the teaching are going well and to modify the approach accordingly.

Hence, the pupil can and should influence the way in which behavioural methods are applied and the techniques need not be exclusively directed by the teacher.

Let us suppose, however, that the teacher alone does make the decision to plan and teach a task using a behavioural approach. Provided he/she is successful in helping the pupil to learn, and provided the pupil enjoys being taught in this way, then it would be churlish to criticize the approach solely because it is the teacher who decides to use it.

Furthermore let us reflect back on our own schooling and ask ourselves how much choice we had over the education we received. Did the teachers spoon-feed or empower us or both? Surely it has been a feature of education over the centuries, long before the introduction of behavioural methods, that teachers imposed their teaching on pupils. Therefore to blame the behavioural approach for allowing teachers to act in this way misses the point.

Behavioural and interactive teaching methods are incompatible and hence, in behaviourally orientated settings, little or no interactive teaching takes place.

Undoubtedly interactive teaching methods, discussed in Chapter 5, have an important part to play in the education of pupils with learning difficulties. However, up until the late 1980s, the literature on learning disability tended to focus on behavioural methods and has played down or ignored the importance of interactive teaching that may have taken place at the same time. As a consequence, it is possible that programme planners may have tended to dwell too much on writing structured teaching programmes and have not stressed the role of interactive teaching. In the last ten years the balance has been redressed (see Smith, 1988, 1991; Nind and Hewett, 1994), reflecting the importance of interactive approaches as well as the use of behavioural methods in pupils' overall programme plans.

Indeed, there is an assumption in the behavioural/interactive dichotomy that the two approaches are mutually exclusive, i.e. that behavioural teaching can never be interactive and that interactive teaching can never be behavioural. This is, of course, over-simplistic. Although behavioural approaches tend to be structured and carefully planned, there is no reason why teachers should not interact less formally during a teaching session. Behavioural techniques such as prompting and rewarding, if done skilfully, can be interactive. Similarly, in less formal group sessions, where interactive teaching is featured more prominently, it is still important to use behavioural techniques such as prompting, reinforcement, shaping, task analysis and many more. Becker (1990) gives an excellent example of how this can be done when using interactive methods to teach language and communication. McConkey (1988) has also shown that it is possible to set clear behavioural targets when teaching interactively. Farrell (1991) and Garner *et al* (1995) provide a more complete discussion of the relationship between behavioural and interactive teaching.

Behavioural approaches rely too heavily on using extrinsic rewards, sometimes food rewards, which are given mechanically and without sincerity.

There is absolutely no doubt that people need regular and immediate feedback (rewards) when learning new tasks. This applies to everyone, including pupils with learning difficulties. We can all think of examples in our own lives of times when our efforts went unrewarded and the effect that had on our feelings and on our ability and willingness to work on a task. For example, if a teacher's hard work in the classroom goes unacknowledged by senior staff in the school then he/she may quickly become disillusioned.

Most people respond to a mixture of extrinsic and intrinsic rewards. For example, we like to be praised and be well paid in our job – extrinsic rewards. We also work hard to engage in a hobby for the pleasure we gain from the activity – intrinsic rewards. When we, as pupils, were introduced to a new task by the teacher – learning to spell twenty unfamiliar words, for example – it is likely that we needed a great deal of extrinsic encouragement to help us. As we became more proficient in essay and story writing, we could see the intrinsic value of learning to spell and hence were not so reliant on the teacher's extrinsic reinforcement to help us to learn. For pupils with and without learning difficulties, many new and important tasks hold no intrinsic interest. Do we refrain from teaching these tasks simply because they are not intrinsically interesting? On the contrary, if everybody thinks that it is important for the pupil to master that particular task or skill, we use extrinsic rewards to help him/her to learn. Hopefully, as the pupil becomes more proficient, the intrinsic value of the task may become apparent and extrinsic rewards may take a less prominent role.

Many pupils with learning difficulties do not respond to the usual extrinsic rewards that operate in our daily lives, particularly those with profound and multiple learning difficulties. Additional and quite inventive rewards may be needed in order to give feedback necessary to encourage learning. Some pupils may not respond to anything other than a food reward and so it may be necessary to use food, otherwise they will not learn. However, even in the most behaviourally orientated settings, food is actually used for very few pupils as the aim is for everybody to learn to respond to more natural social rewards and, in the vast majority of cases, this aim is achieved. Provided we always strive to introduce social rewards and provided we have due regard to pupils' health (by using non-fattening food or drink), the initial use of tangible rewards such as food and drink is justified.

As regards the sincerity of rewards, a really strong social reward may sound insincere but this might not be the way it is perceived by the pupil. We may judge how rewards are perceived by closely observing whether the pupil shows signs of pleasure when receiving the reward and is encouraged to go on working.

Structured behavioural teaching is boring.
This begs the question 'boring for whom'? Pupils do not appear to be bored when they are being taught by someone using a structured one-to-one approach as featured on EDY and Portage programmes. If they appear to be bored, the situation can be improved by changing the task, the setting, the prompts and/or the rewards and by carrying out further task analysis. In this way the teacher remains sensitive to the needs of the pupil.

It is likely that, when people say the approach is boring, they really mean that they, themselves, find it boring to teach in this way. If this is the case, then this feeling may affect the success with which the approach is used and hence the way the student responds. As the approach, used carefully and sensitively, is successful, it is up to teachers to try to keep any feelings of boredom to themselves. Even so, if the work setting is carefully organized, no teacher (or pupil) will be engaged in formal one-to-one teaching all day and hence everybody's activities can be varied and so help reduce the threat of boredom. Classroom management techniques, discussed in Chapter 7, offer strategies for overcoming these problems.

All too often behavioural programmes are taught out of context.
Underlying this statement is the concern that behavioural programmes are frequently taught in a quiet room away from the natural setting where the task, once learned, will be used. For example, is it appropriate to teach a pupil to put on a coat in the classroom in the middle of the day when the coat would not normally be needed? Is it sensible to teach someone to lay the table if it is not time for a meal? It is argued that teaching in the natural context makes learning more meaningful and facilitates generalization. In the above example it is more likely that the pupil will remember the skill of putting on the coat or laying the table if these skills are always taught in context.

Although there is evidence to support this argument (see for example, Haring *et al*, 1988), the main problem lies in the fact that it is not always easy to teach these skills in context as the teacher's attention may be needed elsewhere. For example, if putting on a coat is to be taught in context, i.e. when all the other pupils will be going out, the teacher will need to supervise the whole group, thus making structured teaching with one student almost impossible! In order to practise a task intensively it is quite appropriate to plan a programme and teach it 'out of context' provided opportunities are made for the student to generalize the skill in the appropriate setting. This is compatible with the way we all learn. A musician, for example, will practise a particular phrase of a piece of music over and over again until it has been mastered and will do this 'out of context'. The phrase of music will then be linked together into the main piece so that the whole tune can be played (in context). If teaching has to be done 'out of context', teachers should try and explain to the pupil that they are going to practise the skill so that it can be used in the appropriate context at a later date.

Notwithstanding the above discussion, there is a strong *prima facie* case to teach in context. Possibly one of the most common characteristics of pupils with learning difficulties is the problems they have in generalization and for this reason teaching should take place in natural contexts wherever possible.

The behavioural approach emphasises learning without understanding.
This criticism is related to the previous one. Behind it is the suggestion that pupils learn more effectively if they understand why they

have to learn a task in a particular way. Behavioural methods, it is argued, tend only to focus on what the pupil has to do and not on the reasons why. For example, when teaching someone with learning difficulties to use an electric kettle, behaviourally based teaching programmes only teach the sequence of steps. Explanations about the potential dangers of electricity or boiling water tend not to feature. It is suggested that, if teaching programmes included explanations about these matters, then pupils would learn to use the electric kettle more quickly and safely and there would be a greater chance that, once learned, they would not forget how to use it.

From a theoretical standpoint this argument has much to commend it. However, there are a great many pupils with learning difficulties who are able to learn several tasks but do not have the ability to understand why they have to perform the task in a certain way. Consider the kettle task. The actual steps that need to be learned are relatively straightforward but understanding the way electricity is used to heat up a kettle and its potential dangers is much harder. If we delay teaching the kettle task until the pupil has learned about electricity, we may never teach it. Indeed, it is common for all of us to learn tasks without also understanding the intricate reasons why we have to behave in a certain way to perform the task successfully. For example, we do not need to understand micro technology to learn how to use a word processor.

Like many arguments of this kind, it is possible to arrive at a middle ground. Clearly, as Sebba *et al* (1995) also state, if we fully understand how something works, then it is more likely that we will learn how to use it quickly and effectively. However, in our increasingly technological world, this is not possible and so we learn a great many tasks with only a rudimentary understanding of how and why they work. There is therefore no reason why we should not teach similar tasks to pupils with learning difficulties even if they cannot fully understand the reasons why we need to learn something in a particular way.

Behavioural approaches do not allow the pupil to learn from his/her mistakes.

In the early application of behavioural techniques teachers were encouraged to prompt the pupil quickly so as to prevent mistakes being made, particularly in errorless discrimination learning. It was argued that if the teacher allowed the pupil to make a mistake, he/she would become confused and learning would take longer. It is now recognized that if prompting is delayed, people with learning difficulties can often correct their earlier mistakes and that, as a result, learning is more permanent. Therefore, despite early scepticism, pupils with learning difficulties can solve problems through trial and error learning – see Halle and Touchette (1987) for an excellent discussion of the application of delayed prompting. Indeed, it is the timing of prompts that is crucial to the success of teaching. Some people will work out for themselves how to complete a task and too much prompting may impede this process. Others may get frustrated or learn incorrect behaviours unless they are prompted quickly. If the teacher knows the pupil and task well, there is a greater chance that prompts will be used sensitively. This is one of the skills of being an effective teacher. Of course it should also be stated that there are some tasks where delaying a prompt may be dangerous, for example, in teaching a pupil to cross a road safely.

A behavioural approach is incompatible with normalization.
Some of the key principles of normalization were discussed in Chapter 1. As the philosophy has become more influential, especially in adult services, it has increasingly come to be seen as being in conflict with behavioural methods. While these two approaches do differ in some important respects, many of the criticisms voiced appear to be based on a misunderstanding of both normalization and behavioural methods, a misunderstanding which often reflects people's experience of poor practice.

In essence the extreme views are that normalization, or social role valorization, as it is sometimes called, is equivalent to a policy of radical non-intervention, thus denying people their right to be taught new skills, whereas the critics of the behavioural approach would say that these techniques are dehumanizing and allow for the repressive control of individuals. The idea that the behavioural approach alone runs the risk of transgressing basic human rights is misconceived. Any form of social intervention (including normalization, education etc.) involves questions of who is controlling whom, who selects goals and methods and whose interests does the intervention serve.

Emerson and McGill (1989 a and b) and Emerson (1995) argue that the conflict is more apparent than real and that practitioners should seek to focus on the common factors between the two approaches. An ordinary life philosophy, often associated with principles of normalization, is not incompatible with behavioural methods. A behavioural approach can be harnessed to any goal (for good or evil). Social role valorization provides a conceptual framework which can guide the choice of goals and intervention methods but which does not in itself provide a method of teaching or changing behaviour. Wolfensburger (1972), himself, suggests that 'operant shaping . . . is an approach of vast potential' that 'could be massively injected into our service systems'.

The reality, of course, is that both approaches have a significant and positive contribution to make. With regard to the use of behavioural teaching methods, normalization draws attention to two issues:

1. It stresses the importance of selecting goals which can make an important contribution to pupils' ability to take control over their lives and gain the respect of those around them. These aims are fully consistent with good educational practice built around the need to develop a broad, balanced and relevant curriculum. Furthermore, they may lead us to select goals which build even further upon pupils' unique strengths as well as those which address their disabilities.
2. Normalization draws attention to the details of the teaching procedures which we use. This includes ensuring that the materials are age-appropriate to the person's chronological age, providing as much choice as possible over the learning process and interacting with the pupil in a respectful manner much as we would like the driving instructor, in the example used earlier, to be respectful towards ourselves – even when we make mistakes!

CONCLUSION

This chapter began with a brief review of some of the key principles underpinning the behavioural approach. More detail on how to apply these techniques is provided in Chapters 4 and 5. We then reviewed some of the concerns about the behavioural approach which have been voiced in the last ten years and have shown how they have influenced theory and practice. On the whole these concerns focus on the over-reliance on behavioural methods rather than an outright condemnation. Clearly behavioural methods will always have an important part to play in the effective delivery of services to people with learning difficulties. They should also feature on pre- and in-service courses for staff working in this area. However, they do not provide the whole answer and staff also need to accommodate other approaches.

It is also important to remember that the behavioural approach permeates all our lives. One only has to think about how we all learn new tasks, for example, how to use a word processor, learn a card game, play a musical instrument, in order to recognize the importance of behavioural techniques such as task analysis, prompting, reinforcement and many more. For pupils with learning difficulties these behavioural principles, which govern all our learning, need to be carefully thought out and systematically applied when we plan and implement our teaching programmes in order to ensure that our teaching is successful. The well-known saying, 'If you don't know where you are going, how will you know when you have got there?', is particularly apt in relation to the importance of the behavioural approach. Indeed, there is now abundant evidence (see, for example, Haring *et al*, 1988, and from the international success of the Portage project) that if these techniques are applied sensitively, pupils with severe learning difficulties can learn many new skills and enjoy being taught in this way.

Behavioural techniques therefore represent *one* very important set of skills which help teachers plan and carry out teaching programmes successfully. However, the *first* priority when deciding on a teaching programme is to agree on the pupil's overall needs and to select those areas from the whole curriculum which are relevant for that person to learn. Only when this has been done should one then choose the appropriate teaching method. Structured behavioural techniques will almost certainly be applicable, particularly when teaching new skills and knowledge. There may be some areas, however, where behavioural methods form only a part of the teaching method used.

CHAPTER 4

Planning teaching programmes

INTRODUCTION

This chapter and the next focus on ways of planning and implementing teaching programmes when working with individuals and small groups of pupils with learning difficulties. In this chapter we shall focus on key factors to consider when planning teaching programmes, while the next chapter covers some specific teaching strategies. Both chapters have been adapted from the Education of the Developmentally Young (EDY) training materials (McBrien, Farrell and Foxen, 1992; Farrell, McBrien and Foxen, 1992) although Chapter 5 also includes a discussion of the application of interactive teaching and on the importance of group work.

Both chapters take as their starting point the belief that in order to help pupils with learning difficulties to learn, teaching has to be carefully planned and much of it may need to be done on a one-to-one or small group basis. Generally, the greater the learning difficulty, the greater the amount of careful planning is required and the greater the amount of one-to-one or small group teaching is needed. Individual teaching is therefore an important aspect of the whole process of education and development and should form part of an overall teaching plan.

The theoretical routes which underpin the techniques featured in these chapters lie in behavioural psychology. Behavioural approaches to teaching pupils with learning difficulties have been extremely influential all over the world for many years. As the chapters illustrate, used sensitively, behavioural techniques help all pupils to learn new skills and knowledge and are not restricted to those who have learning difficulties. However, as we have seen in the previous chapter, behavioural methods are not without their critics and in recent years, in particular, many authors have questioned the over-reliance on behavioural teaching which has been observed in some schools, the fact that the approach is often teacher-led, too directive and does not allow pupils enough choice over what they do. Further criticisms have been levelled at behaviourally based curricula for being too narrow and inflexible and at teaching programmes for being carried out in unfamiliar contexts which leads to problems of generalization.

Critics of behavioural teaching methods do acknowledge, however, that the approach continues to have an important part to play in teaching pupils with learning difficulties provided they are combined with other approaches. Indeed, the concerns they raise are primarily about the inappropriate way in which the approach has been applied in some schools, apparently to the exclusion of all other methods.

In Chapter 3 we illustrated the role that behavioural techniques play in teaching people to learn to drive and showed that the driving instructor, possibly without knowing it, is using standard behavioural teaching techniques such as *establishing a baseline, target behaviour, task analysis, modelling, prompting and reinforcement.* These techniques, and others, are discussed in this and the following chapter. There are, in fact, a great many skills which we all learn during our lives which are taught using the same methods as those that are used when teaching someone to drive a car. Learning to type, cook, wire an electric plug, play a musical instrument, are some other examples. Obviously the more complex the task, the more planning is required and the more systematic the teaching should be; the principles of the behavioural approach feature in the way we all learn and they are not restricted to pupils with learning difficulties.

However, for pupils with learning difficulties a systematically applied teaching programme is required to teach many skills that other people learn easily. For example, most pupils learn to dress as a result of some relatively straightforward task analysis, prompting, modelling and rewarding. These behavioural approaches do not usually need to be applied in a particularly systematic way for the vast majority of pupils. However, for the pupil with learning difficulties it may be necessary for a teacher or parent to give a great deal of thought to teaching one single aspect of dressing, for example putting on a sock. There are a great many similar skills that pupils with learning difficulties need to learn which can be taught by systematically applying the teaching techniques featured in these chapters.

This chapter and the next are therefore 'How to teach' chapters in that they focus on teaching techniques that can be applied to almost all areas of the curriculum for pupils with learning difficulties both in individual and small group teaching. We do not focus directly on curriculum development itself as this is covered in Chapter 6. Furthermore Fagg *et al* (1990), Ashdown *et al* (1991), Tilstone (1991), Sebba *et al* (1995), Coupe-O'Kane and Smith (1994) and Carpenter *et al* (1996) all discuss curriculum issues in some depth, in particular the relevance of the National Curriculum for pupils with severe learning difficulties.

This chapter is divided into the following sections, each of which is concerned with how to plan teaching programmes:

- antecedents and setting conditions;
- writing clear targets for teaching;
- baselines;
- task analysis.

ANTECEDENTS AND SETTING CONDITIONS

An essential feature of the behavioural approach is understanding how 'antecedents', 'setting conditions' and 'consequences' influence 'behaviour' . In this section we introduce these terms and concentrate on the role of *antecedents* and *setting conditions*. There is more detailed discussion on behaviour and consequences later in this chapter and the next.

Behaviour is anything which we do or say which other people can observe. A behaviour is anything from simple events, such as blinking or walking, to complex chains of behaviour such as making coffee, driving a car, writing a letter, speaking on the telephone. When teaching someone with learning difficulties we pay great attention to defining the behaviour we wish to teach. This is covered in detail in the next section.

Antecedents are the triggers to behaviour. Behaviour does not occur in isolation. We do not sleep, eat, talk, work, drive a car, sneeze, etc., for no reason. There is always something which occurs immediately before the behaviour which is responsible for setting it off. The events which occur before a behaviour are called the *antecedents*. For example, the antecedent to the behaviour of 'sleeping' may be 'tiredness'. The antecedent to 'eating' may be 'the sight of food'. The antecedent to 'talking' may be that 'someone has asked us a question'.

Setting conditions provide the context for the antecedent and the behaviour that follows. For example 'tiredness' may occur at night just before bed time. In this case the behaviour of 'sleeping' is appropriate. This context 'just before bed time' is called the *setting condition*. The same antecedent of 'tiredness' could occur in a different setting condition, for example whilst driving along a motorway.

In this setting condition the behaviour of 'sleeping' would be inappropriate, even though the *antecedent* of 'tiredness' is the same.

Consequences are whatever follow behaviour. There is always a consequence of some kind. Some consequences are pleasant and these are called reinforcers; some consequences are unpleasant and these are called punishers. It is a basic law of learning that the consequences of behaviour determine the likelihood of our behaving in the same way again. The term 'reinforcement' refers to pleasant consequences which strengthen behaviour and make it more likely to happen again.

A consequence which is unpleasant and not desirable is known technically as a 'punisher'. For example, if the telephone rings (antecedent), we answer it (behaviour) and there is an obscene caller on the other end (consequence), this consequence acts as a punisher and makes us less likely to answer the telephone next time it rings. In this and the following chapter we are not concerned with punishers except to give us a general understanding of their possible effects on behaviour. *The best way to teach new behaviour is to use reinforcers (i.e. desirable consequences).* The consequences of behaviour, in particular the use of rewards, will be considered in more detail in the next chapter.

The basic point to remember is that all learning and behaviour does not occur in a vacuum. Both are directly influenced by the setting conditions, antecedents and consequences. By observing all three carefully we increase the chance that we can not only understand existing behaviour, but also teach new behaviours. This applies to us all, whether or not we have learning difficulties.

Antecedents and their effects on learning

Learning new skills relies in part on the child coming to recognize the meaning of the antecedents. When you first present a small child with a potty (antecedent), it is very unlikely that the potty will be seen as something to sit on and 'perform in'. The antecedent of seeing the potty has no meaning. When teaching a child to use the potty appropriately we have to pair the appearance of the potty with the behaviour of using it. For example we might place a child on the potty immediately after a meal (a favourable setting condition) and then reward the child for using it. Gradually the child will learn that the sight of the potty (antecedent) is a signal to urinate (behaviour).

It can sometimes take a long time for pupils with learning

difficulties to learn how to respond appropriately to an antecedent. For example, a pupil with profound and multiple learning difficulties may have difficulty learning to associate the call of his or her name (antecedent) with the desired behaviour, e.g. a smile or turn of the head in acknowledgement, and with the consequence of the behaviour (reward), e.g. a smile, cuddle, praise.

In the above examples the aim is to teach the pupil to respond to new and unfamiliar antecedents. However a great deal of behaviour occurs without ever having been taught and it is not always easy to see what the antecedents are that influence it. For example, parents may wonder why their baby is crying. Frequently they go through a series of possible reasons (antecedents) e.g. the baby is hungry, tired, teething, got a wet nappy, is too hot, too cold, and so on. The parents learn by repeated experience and careful observation which situations (antecedents) lead to crying.

Pupils with learning difficulties may not have the ability to tell us about the antecedents which affect their behaviour, particularly 'internal' antecedents such as a headache. Finding out what these are is a matter of careful observation. If we fail to do this we may respond to the behaviour inappropriately. For example a pupil with the headache may sit quietly and not want to join in an activity. We may not have noticed this feeling of discomfort and we may respond by trying to make the pupil join in, hence probably making the situation worse.

The effect of setting conditions

Setting conditions affect the way we all behave including, of course, the way we work with pupils with learning difficulties. If we arrive at work having had a row with our partner (an addition to the usual combination of setting conditions associated with work), our response (behaviour) when a member of a group for whom we are responsible asks us a question (antecedent) may be irritable and hostile. This may adversely affect the whole group by making them unpleasant in return. This then becomes a further antecedent which may possibly make us even more bad tempered with the group. It is important to remember that we may not always be aware of how our own problems may contribute to the setting conditions and that this may influence the way we behave at work and hence the behaviour of the people for whom we are responsible.

Pupils with learning difficulties are affected by changes in setting conditions like everybody else. Some may be affected by dramatic changes in weather conditions, or by a change of class teacher, others may not be. Only careful observation may reveal this. When working with somebody it is always necessary to consider the range of possible setting conditions which might influence the likelihood that learning will take place. For instance a pupil may be more receptive to teaching in the morning than in the afternoon. Equally, a distractible person may work better in a quiet room than a noisy one. Someone who has recently been given a tranquillizer is likely to be less responsive to teaching. The drug in the bloodstream is the setting condition for poorer performance.

This last paragraph is particularly important in view of the recent emphasis on the need to teach pupils with learning difficulties in natural contexts, that is in setting conditions where the skill or task they are learning is likely to be used. For example, is it sensible to teach a pupil to lay the table when it is not time for dinner? Should we teach pupils to name objects when this activity is not part of a natural and spontaneous conversation? There is a large body of evidence (see Haring *et al*, 1988) that pupils with learning difficulties generalize their learning more effectively if they are taught in 'natural contexts'. This is likely to make the task more meaningful to the pupil and will therefore increase his or her interest in learning it. We will return to this point in the next chapter when we discuss ways of helping pupils with learning difficulties to generalize their learning.

WRITING TARGETS FOR TEACHING

As stated earlier, this chapter and the next focus on developing *teaching techniques* which can be applied to almost all areas of learning. They do not consider how you decide what you will teach and wider issues concerned with curriculum development. Nevertheless it is *vitally important* to teach targets which are necessary for the pupil to learn; they should fit in with the overall long-term goals as established by the school and family. The pupil should be involved in the selection of targets wherever possible. Teachers and pupils put in a great deal of time and effort working on the selected goals, so it is important to avoid trivial, unimportant targets or ones which can never be put into practice later.

When planning teaching programmes it is important to be clear about what it is that is being taught and when learning has taken place. This applies for all pupils, including those with learning difficulties. The saying (also referred to in Chapter 3) 'If you do not know where you are going, how will you know when you have got there?' is very relevant in this context. For many years schools for pupils with learning difficulties have been expert in writing clear target behaviours when planning their teaching programmes and although this approach has been criticized as being too rigid and not appropriate for some curriculum areas (see for example Harris, 1988), other writers have still stressed its importance (see for example, NCC, 1992; Coupe-O'Kane and Baker, 1993; Byers, 1994).

Target behaviours should state what the student will be able to do when the task has been mastered. They should be described as precisely as possible. One way of doing this is to follow the structure for writing behavioural objectives. (The terms 'behavioural objective' and 'target behaviour' refer to the same thing.) Target behaviours should be written in such a way that they contain the following elements:

- A statement of 'who will do what'.
- The conditions under which the pupil is expected to perform the task.
- The criterion of success.

Who will do what. A behavioural objective must state exactly 'what' the pupil should be able to do. A helpful way of doing this is to make sure that it contains an 'observable verb'. Target behaviours should contain verbs like 'says', 'writes', 'walks', 'points to'. Having written a target behaviour, it should be possible to visualize how one might observe the pupil performing the task once it has been mastered. If it will not be possible to do this, then the chances are that an observable verb has not been included in the target behaviour. Instead a 'fuzzy' instead of a clear verb may have been used. Fuzzies are words and phrases such as 'increase his potential', 'become more polite', 'understand money'.

The conditions under which the pupil is expected to perform the task, for example:

- The setting in which the pupil is expected to learn the task, e.g. in the classroom, the home, the toilet or at the shop.
- The materials that are required.
- How the instructions are to be given by the teacher, e.g. verbally or with a demonstration.
- How much help, if any, should be given.

The criterion of success. Having defined a target behaviour, it is also important to decide how proficient the pupil should be at performing it in order to be certain that he/she has really learnt it. For instance, few of us would say that a pupil had learned to select a 20p coin from a pocketful of change if he/she had only done this correctly on one occasion out of ten. Similarly, we would not say that a pupil with learning difficulties had learned to travel independently on a bus from home to school if this had only been achieved twice out of six attempts. The criterion of success is the number of times the student must carry out the target behaviour successfully before we all agree that it has been mastered. The criterion of success, set at the beginning of the teaching programme, must reflect the level of mastery required for the task to be performed satisfactorily. The precise level of mastery depends on:

- *The nature of the task.* Tasks where failure to perform satisfactorily might put the pupil in danger (e.g. using a cooker) require a stricter criterion of success than tasks where failure to perform accurately carries no risk, e.g. eating with a spoon.
- *The pupil's previous performance on similar tasks.* For example a pupil who is known to have a poor memory may require a much stricter criterion of success than a pupil who retains information easily.

Examples of target behaviours:

- John will pull down his trousers and pants in the toilet and urinate in the toilet bowl, without help, when asked 'John, can you go to the toilet?', 3/3 times correct each day for a week.
- Tracy will look at the teacher for one second when asked 'Tracy, look at me' on eight out of ten trials.
- Ataf will point to a 5p coin (from a randomly arranged group of coins containing a 1p, 2p, 5p, 10p, 20p and 50p) when asked to do so by his teacher, five out of five times.

In the above examples the setting has only been specified for John as it would clearly be inappropriate for him to take his trousers and pants off in any other setting when asked to go to the toilet. In the other two examples it does not matter a great deal where the teaching takes place. Even so it would probably be better to teach Tracy to 'look at her teacher' in a quiet area free from too many distractions. Similarly Ataf may initially learn to identify coins more successfully in a quiet setting, although it would be important for him to learn to generalize this activity to a shop.

Clearly then, for some target behaviours, it is important to be specific about the setting in which teaching should take place while for others it may not matter so much.

BASELINES

Having decided on the target behaviour, it is essential to assess how well the pupil can carry out the skill (if at all) before teaching begins. For example, if the target behaviour is for the pupil to eat with a spoon, he/she should be observed attempting to eat, possibly with a variety of different sizes of spoon. It may be that he/she can already perform parts of this task, or that it is much too difficult and that eating with fingers would be a better starting point. Finding out how well someone can perform a task is called finding the baseline.

The baseline may confirm that the choice of target behaviour exactly suits the needs of the pupil. However it may suggest that the target behaviour should be adapted or scrapped altogether, because it is too easy or too difficult. The pupil's performance on a baseline may also provide ideas about how the task materials should be arranged to facilitate teaching and learning. There are many ways of establishing baselines. The simplest is to set up the necessary materials, ask the student to begin, watch closely and make notes.

TASK ANALYSIS

Up to now we have stressed the importance of setting clear target behaviours and carrying out baselines when planning teaching programmes. However, even an apparently simple target behaviour may be very complicated for a pupil with learning difficulties to learn unless we break it down into smaller steps; this is called *task analysis*. Careful task analysis helps the student to master the task step by step. In this way learning is more likely to occur because small steps can be achieved and rewarded. In addition, the teacher can see clearly how much progress is being made.

There are two main stages we must go through when analysing a task. First, describe the target behaviour exactly. Second, describe the steps leading to the target behaviour. These steps should include all parts of the task which are necessary for the pupil to reach the target behaviour. The final task analysis will depend on the nature of the task, on the teacher's knowledge of the pupil and on how he/she performs on a few baseline trials. The same task may well be analysed differently for different pupils.

Example of a task analysis: using an electric kettle

Target behaviour: when presented with an empty electric kettle (Figure 4.1) and asked to fill it up to the 'maximum' mark, plug it in and switch it on, the pupil completes the task correctly once a day for a week.

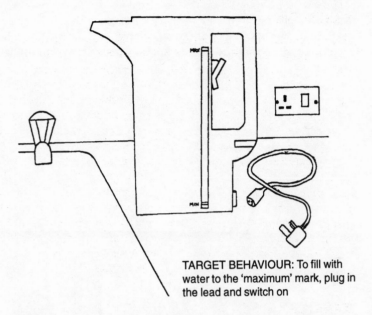

TARGET BEHAVIOUR: To fill with
water to the 'maximum' mark, plug in
the lead and switch on

Figure 4.1:   Using a 'jug' kettle (taken from McBrien *et al*, 1992)

Figure 4.1 shows the kettle, the lead lying next to it, the electric
socket and the sink. For this task analysis the exact position of these
objects is not important provided the pupil knows where the sink and
the socket are. Figure 4.2 illustrates one way to analyse this task into
small steps – five in this case. There are other ways to analyse the
same task.

Although each step could be taught on its own, in order for the
pupil to learn how the whole task is linked together, it is important
for each new step to incorporate the previous ones. Hence when
working on Step 2, placing the lead into the kettle, the pupil would
also incorporate Step 1, filling the kettle with water.

When planning a task analysis it is important to consider whether
it is essential to keep to the order of steps or not. Some steps may have
to be done before others (e.g. for safety reasons), for other steps there
may be a choice. During the *baseline* the pupil may show an inclina-
tion to learn the steps in a particular order, different from the one
planned. This may be fine, in which case re-order the task analysis.
Once the order of steps has been finalized, it should be adhered to and
all people who teach the pupil should work through the steps in the
agreed order.

Teaching step by step. When the task analysis has been finalized, teaching should begin on a step-by-step basis. As with setting clear target behaviours, it is important to set a criterion of success for each step of the task so that the teacher knows when to move on to the next step.

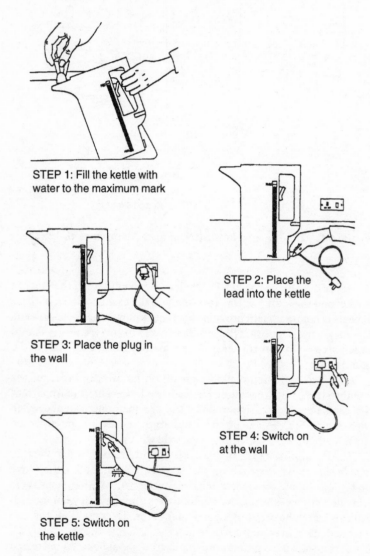

STEP 1: Fill the kettle with water to the maximum mark

STEP 2: Place the lead into the kettle

STEP 3: Place the plug in the wall

STEP 4: Switch on at the wall

STEP 5: Switch on the kettle

Figure 4.2: **Task analysis for using a 'jug' kettle (taken from McBrien *et al*, 1992)**

What to do if the pupil is having difficulty in learning the task

There may be several reasons why pupils may have difficulty learning the task or one step of it. For example:

- The pupil may be confused due to the task not being presented clearly – the materials may be in a muddle or the teacher may be distracting the student by using inappropriate language.
- The pupil may be finding the whole teaching session unrewarding resulting in him/her losing interest or appearing fed up.
- The step may be too difficult.

The following are some suggested solutions:

1. The teacher should observe carefully whether, i) the pupil is attending to the task; ii) the materials are set out correctly and there are no distractions; iii) the instructions are clear; iv) the prompting is effective (see the next chapter for a discussion of prompting).
2. If the above does not work, the teacher should go back to the previous step which has already been learned. If the pupil fails on this step as well, then perhaps the student has forgotten how to do it and it needs to be taught again, possibly to a stricter criterion of success.
3. If the pupil succeeds on the previous step, the problem may lie in the present step being too difficult. The teacher could do further task analysis on this step and break it down into two or more simpler steps.
4. Perhaps the pupil no longer feels rewarded for working on the task. In this case, a different reward could be used or existing rewards could be strengthened (see the next chapter for a discussion on the use of rewards). Alternatively the pupil could be given a break from working on the task.

SUMMARY

In this chapter we have reviewed some of the main factors to consider when planning teaching programmes for pupils with learning difficulties. The main points are as follows:

1. Learning (defined here as *behaviour* that indicates that we have learned something) is affected by the environment in which teaching takes place (*setting conditions*), by how specific teaching

activities are taught (*antecedents*), and by the *consequences* (reinforcers or punishers).

2. It is not always possible to observe the antecedents or the relevant components of the setting conditions which may be influencing other people's behaviour, in particular pupils with learning difficulties.

3. It is important to understand how setting conditions and antecedents can affect our behaviour towards pupils who have learning difficulties.

4. When planning a teaching programme it is important to set clear target behaviours.

5. Before finalizing the programme, we should carry out a baseline to see how the student approaches the task.

6. Many things that we want to teach are too complicated to learn in one step and need to be broken down into smaller steps. This is referred to as task analysis.

7. We can break down any task in this way however simple or complex it appears.

CHAPTER 5

Developing teaching techniques

INTRODUCTION

In the previous chapter we discussed key factors related to planning teaching programmes: antecedents, setting conditions, target behaviours, baselines and task analysis. In this chapter we shall focus on how to teach programmes successfully. In particular we shall discuss the use of rewards, prompting, and forward and backward training. We shall also consider the importance of encouraging generalization, of developing effective group work and of interactive approaches.

THE USE OF REWARDS

Put very simply a *reinforcer* (*reward*) is something we like. As most of us like many things, there is an enormous number of rewards which work for us. However, as we are all unique as individuals, the rewards to which one person responds are not always the same as those for another person. Most children like sweets and most adults like money. Some children like sport, but some do not. Some adults like gardening while others would prefer to do something else. Each person's range of rewards is unique.

When we behave in a certain way and, as a consequence, are given something we like, then our behaviour has been reinforced. If we are reinforced, we are likely to behave in the same way again and hence learning occurs. If we are not reinforced, then we are less likely to behave in the same way and learning will not occur.

Consider the following example. If we make a special effort to cook a nice meal, we will hopefully be pleased with the outcome and those who eat it will thank us and offer to do the washing up! Hence our efforts are rewarded and we are more likely to make a special effort to make a nice meal in the future. However, if something went wrong when cooking the meal or if it was not appreciated, then our efforts go unrewarded and we are less likely to make the same special

effort again. Hence actions which lead to pleasant outcomes are reinforced (strengthened) and those which lead to unpleasant outcomes
are not.

Over the years research has shown that people learn more effectively and enjoyably when the emphasis is on reinforcement.
Therefore this chapter emphasises the importance of using *reinforcement* when teaching, in this case the giving of pleasant consequences
(*rewards*) for behaviour we want someone to learn (*the target behaviour*).

Extrinsic and intrinsic rewards

An extrinsic reward is one which is provided by someone else. Praise,
a hug, money, toys, are examples of extrinsic rewards. Intrinsic
rewards are not provided by someone else, but come from 'within' the
person being rewarded. The personal pleasure we may get from playing tennis, or the satisfaction of doing a job well are examples of
intrinsic rewards.

Consider a parent who asks a child to tidy his/her bedroom and
promises ice cream with dinner as a reward. The ice cream is an
extrinsic reward given by the parent. However, it is possible that
eventually the child will see the benefit of having a tidy room and feel
more comfortable in it. This is the intrinsic reward. At first the child
may only tidy the room because of the ice cream but gradually this
extrinsic reward will not be necessary as the intrinsic reward of having a tidy room becomes more important.

When we start to learn something new, particularly a task about
which we are apprehensive, we tend to need extrinsic rewards more,
e.g. someone to encourage and praise us. But as we start to master the
task, intrinsic rewards should take over. Nevertheless we always
need some extrinsic rewards. For example we may really enjoy our
work (intrinsic reward) but if the boss never appreciates our efforts, or
if the salary is low (extrinsic rewards), we may soon cease to be enthusiastic about it.

Finding out what serves as a reward

As using rewards systematically helps people to learn, it is important
when working with a pupil who has learning difficulties, to know
what rewards to use. Ideally we should use natural social rewards
such as praise and for the majority of pupils this will be sufficient.
However, some pupils with learning difficulties do not respond to
praise and alternative methods may be needed. They may also be
unable to tell us which rewards they would like.

The most effective way of finding out what is rewarding for a pupil is to get to know him/her well, and through this find out what kind of things he/she likes as these may be used as rewards. The more closely we work with someone, the better our judgements will become and in this way it is usually possible to decide on the most appropriate rewards to use.

An alternative method is to place a few likely rewards in front of the pupil and observe which is chosen. Examples of such rewards could be a piece of cake, a small toy or a drink, a notebook, a purse and a clock. If we put three such objects in front of the pupil several times we can find out which one is preferred by observing which is selected. This may then be tried as a reward when teaching, although there is no guarantee that it will work. The teacher will only be able to find out by working with the pupil.

However, not all potential rewards can be put in front of a pupil at the same time. Social rewards can only be tried one after the other. We cannot give someone a simultaneous choice between a hug on the one hand and our saying 'That's good!' on the other. Nor can we give a simultaneous choice between a toy and 'That's good!' If we use other kinds of experience for rewards, such as music or showing a picture, we find ourselves with the same problem. In this case we could present potential rewards one after the other in order to see what effect they have. We would show each in turn a number of times and observe signs of pleasure such as smiling, attempts to reach the reward or increased movement. Again our experience of the pupil will tell us what to look for.

Even when we think we have established which rewards the pupil likes, we can only make sure that one of them works by finding out if the pupil responds to it in a teaching situation.

'Age-appropriate' rewards

Age-appropriate rewards are rewards which are appropriate to use for any person of a given age regardless of disability. Social rewards, such as praise, are almost always appropriate, so long as we avoid addressing adults as 'Good boy' or 'Good girl'. It may be appropriate to reward a 4-year-pupil with a sweet and a cuddle but not a 21-year-old. We need to ask ourselves whether it looks or feels 'right' to offer a particular reward to an individual who has learning difficulties.

Generally the more intrinsically interesting the task and the more able the pupil, the less need there is to use anything other than social rewards to encourage learning. However there are many tasks which are of no immediate intrinsic interest to the pupil but which are nevertheless important to learn. This is particularly true of people with learning difficulties. In these cases it may be necessary to use a non-age-appropriate reward such as a sweet or a cuddle as these may be the only ones to which the pupil responds. Without the use of these rewards the person may not learn. One has to weigh up the balance between the importance of the task with the appropriateness of the reward needed to teach it. If the task is vital, but of no obvious intrinsic interest to the pupil, then we may have to use non-age-appropriate extrinsic rewards. Recently this debate has been highlighted by Nind and Hewett (1996) who strongly advocate using non-age-appropriate rewards with people with profound and multiple learning difficulties in order to help them develop communication skills, one of the aims of intensive interaction. We will discuss interactive teaching methods later in this chapter, and the issue of age-appropriateness is also reviewed in Chapter 6.

Using extrinsic rewards: three rules

There are three rules that should be followed when giving extrinsic rewards to pupils with learning difficulties. They should be given immediately, enthusiastically and consistently. These rules are discussed in more detail below.

Immediate rewarding. College students will usually work harder if they receive feedback and reinforcement as soon as possible after their assignments have been completed. The same is true for pupils with learning difficulties. Indeed, it may be important for the reward to be given within one second of the person doing what is required. It must be clear what the reward is for. If we delay the reward, then we may be rewarding some other behaviour and the person will not associate the reward with the work which has been completed and hence may be less likely to work on the same activity again. If, for example, we are teaching a pupil with profound and multiple learning difficulties to pick up a cup unaided, the task may be completed successfully but the cup then dropped on the floor. If we do not reward immediately the cup has been picked up, we will have rewarded the pupil for dropping the cup on the floor.

Enthusiastic reward. Learning will proceed more rapidly if we use rewards enthusiastically. If, for example, the pupil is rewarded by physical contact, then it is likely that a really affectionate cuddle will be more rewarding than a pat on the back. Rewards should be rewarding – not just gestures to show that the pupil is correct. This is especially true if the task holds no intrinsic interest for the pupil or if we are teaching a particularly difficult part of it.

Consistency of reward. At the start of teaching a new task, rewards should be given every time the student completes a trial. When he/she begins to master it, it may be feasible to reward less frequently, and later still, only at the end of a teaching session.

These three rules of giving extrinsic rewards are especially important when teaching new or difficult parts of a task and/or when a task holds no intrinsic interest for the pupil. It is also important for the reward to gain the pupil's attention. If the pupil fails to notice the reward right away then this will have the same effect as delaying it. He/she will not associate the reward with the behaviour we are trying to teach. For the same reasons, it is better to use the strongest reward possible.

As the pupil becomes interested in the task and starts to master it, the need for strength and consistency of rewards decreases. However it is vital to remember that, even when we feel we can relax the strict rules referred to above, extrinsic rewards continue to play an important part in the way we all learn and should always be used.

Using more than one reward

There is no reason why more than one reward should not be used. This can increase the attention-getting value of the reward and ensure that the effect is a strong one. If one reward is more immediate than another, then, by presenting it immediately and following it with the other one, we can reduce the effects of delaying the second one. It is also possible to vary the kind of rewards used in a teaching session. This can help to maintain the pupil's attention by introducing variety. It can also offset the effect of the pupil receiving too much of a particular reward (satiation effect) – a problem particularly likely when we use food.

PROMPTING

We use prompting to help pupils learn a difficult or unfamiliar part of a task and to remind them about parts of a task which they have previously learned and have temporarily forgotten.

The types of prompts which can be used reflect the degree of help that the pupil needs. Physical prompting involves a lot of help. Gestural and verbal prompting involve less help. Whatever prompts are used it is important to give feedback by rewarding the pupil so as to encourage him/her to try again. The various types of prompting are discussed below.

Physical prompting

Physical prompting means manually guiding the pupil through those parts of the task which are difficult to perform. The teacher actually holds the pupil's hand or wrist and physically guides the limbs through the movements involved. This may range from a simple action such as waving 'Bye bye', to a more complex task such as writing one's name.

In physical prompting, the teacher must become sensitive to the pupil's movement and steer it. In order to do this, the teacher needs to be ready to prompt, shadowing the pupil's hand at a short distance. At no stage should the teacher touch the materials as this will prevent the pupil from getting the feel of how to use them.

It is important to note that physical prompting is not designed to force people to do something they do not want to do. If the pupil actively resists prompting, we should review the task in case it is too difficult, or review the rewards we are using. There are some pupils with learning difficulties who do not like being touched under any circumstances and in these cases physical prompting must be used very carefully and alternatives found where possible.

Gestural prompting

Gestural prompting involves actions by the teacher which indicate to the pupil what is required. For example, the teacher may indicate what is required by pointing to the relevant materials. More help may be given by moving the hand(s) in a manner demonstrating the action to be performed or the object to be selected. For example, the teacher may make a drinking gesture when asking someone to drink from a cup; or the teacher may point to the plug and then to the socket to indicate that the person is expected to put the plug in the socket.

A more sophisticated form of gestural prompt is eye pointing which can be used to indicate a particular object to be picked up or where it is to be placed.

Verbal prompting

When teaching, the instruction to begin a task (i.e. the presentation) may be repeated and act as a verbal prompt to encourage the student to continue with the task. Indeed any verbal instruction or request which *follows* the initial presentation of a task can be referred to as a verbal prompt. Most of us can learn new tasks by being given clear verbal prompts (for example the driving instructor can effectively shout 'Brake' and most people respond to this verbal prompt appropriately).

The complexity of the verbal prompt should reflect the pupil's ability to understand language – staff should not make the mistake of using words or sentences which the pupil cannot comprehend. Prompts should help pupils to learn and this is less likely to occur if the verbal prompts (or the instructions) are complex and above the pupil's level of comprehension. If the pupil does not respond to a verbal prompt, then it is more effective to use gestural and physical prompting than to carry on repeating verbal prompts which are not responded to.

When using verbal prompts alone it is important to be sure that we are not inadvertently using gestural prompts as well. For example, a pupil may respond to changes in facial expression, to the direction the teacher's eyes are pointing or to where the teacher's hand happens to be resting. These are all forms of unintentional gestural prompts of which we may be unaware at the time. Unless we can become aware of our non-verbal cues or gestures we cannot be sure that the pupil is only responding to our verbal prompts.

Fading prompts

We say that a pupil has learned something when a new task or part of it can be performed without help. The aim of prompting is to help the pupil so that he/she will eventually work unaided. Therefore, before we can say that the pupil has learned, the prompts must be gradually withdrawn. This is described as fading the prompt. The method of fading is from greatest to least assistance, i.e. physical prompts are faded first, then gestural and finally verbal prompts.

The timing of prompts

When teaching someone a new task it is helpful to know the pupil well so that the teacher is familiar with the speed at which he/she usually works. If the pupil generally works at a slow but steady pace, it is important not to prompt too early but to give the pupil a chance to respond without help. For pupils who work more quickly, delaying a prompt may result in them losing interest in the task or becoming confused by their mistakes. Hence the timing of prompts is crucial. Delaying prompts encourages the pupil to solve problems unaided. If this is successful, it may increase the chances that what is learned will not be forgotten. However, delaying the prompt should be used very cautiously. Pupils with learning difficulties tend not to learn by problem-solving but need consistent teaching to master everyday tasks. If left unprompted, the pupil may not learn the task at all and could become bored or upset by failure. Strong, extrinsic rewards will help to motivate the pupil and so it is often important to prompt quickly so that the reward can be given.

There is no correct way of deciding when it is time to prompt. Only by knowing the pupil well and by carefully observing their responses when working on the task will a teacher be able to judge when a prompt is needed. As a general rule it is a better to over-prompt at the beginning of a new task and then fade the prompts rather than delay prompting in the belief the student will somehow get it right without being shown.

FORWARD AND BACKWARD TRAINING

The following is a description of a task analysis for putting on a coat. It is given as an example to help explain what is meant by forward and backward training. (Obviously there are many ways to analyse such tasks and the precise task analysis which would be used in a teaching programme for a particular pupil would depend on the type of coat that he/she was supposed to wear and on the characteristics of the pupil. In addition each of the steps could be broken down into smaller steps).

Step 1   Pick up the coat at the correct point.
Step 2   Put one arm in the correct sleeve.
Step 3   Put the other arm in.
Step 4   Pull the coat up round the shoulders.
Step 5   Fasten the zip.

Forward training

If we were to teach the pupil using forward training we would start by teaching him/her to pick up the coat at the correct point (step 1). When the criterion of success had been reached we would teach the next step which should incorporate the first one so that the pupil is learning a sequence of steps. Therefore step 2 (putting one arm in the correct sleeve) includes step 1 (picking up the coat at the correct point). When the criterion of success had been reached on this step, we would move on to teach step 3 (putting the other arm in), always remembering that steps 1 and 2 should be incorporated into this new step. Eventually when we reach the final step (step 5) the pupil will be completing the whole task (i.e. the target behaviour – steps 1 to 5). We call this method forward training as the pupil starts at the beginning and moves progressively forward through the task. The order of teaching the steps is the same as the task analysis.

Backward training

If we were to teach the pupil to put on the coat using backward training we would first help the pupil to put the coat on until we got as far as the zip which we would then ask him/her to fasten. In this way fastening the zip becomes step 1 and our task analysis is as follows.

Step 1   Fasten the zip.
Step 2   Pull the coat up round the shoulders.
Step 3   Put the second arm in the sleeve.
Step 4   Put one arm in the correct sleeve.
Step 5   Pick up the coat at the correct point.

In step 2 the pupil has to pull the coat round the shoulders and fasten the zip (i.e. complete steps 1 and 2). In step 3 the pupil puts the second arm in the sleeve, pulls the coat round the shoulders and fastens the zip (i.e. completes steps 1, 2 and 3).

This method of teaching is called backward training as the pupil starts at the 'end' of the task (in this example by fastening the zip) and the teaching steps are in the reverse order to the way they normally occur.

Deciding when to use forward or backward training

For pupils with learning difficulties backward training is frequently the preferred method of teaching. The advantage of backward training is that the pupil always completes the task after each trial. This means that the task as a whole should have more meaning and that the reward can be given at the natural point (i.e. for completion of the target) and not at an arbitrary point part-way through (e.g. a reward for picking up the coat). In the above example of backward training, starting by teaching the pupil to fasten the zip carries with it the immediate reward of the coat being put on and is generally a more meaningful activity than just picking it up (the first step in the forward training sequence). Similarly when teaching a young pupil to assemble a constructional toy, teaching the last step first makes it easier to see how the completed toy will look and hence is likely to be more intrinsically rewarding. The first step may bear no resemblance to the completed toy and hence teaching it first may not be particularly rewarding and so extrinsic rewards will need to be strong in order to keep the pupil motivated.

However, there are many tasks, e.g. learning to play a musical instrument, which can only be taught through forward training. Suppose the target behaviour is for a pupil to play the tune 'Happy

Birthday' on the recorder. The teacher has to use a forward training procedure, the exact sequence of which would depend on the pupil's performance on a series of baseline trials.

GENERALIZATION AND DISCRIMINATION

If a pupil has been taught to use the toilet correctly at school but does not use it at home, he/she has failed to *generalize* the skill from one setting to the other. Similarly if a pupil hugs all adults he/she meets, it is clear that there is a failure to *discriminate* between those people it is appropriate to hug (e.g. his or her parents) and those it is not. Many pupils with learning difficulties have problems in learning to discriminate between the setting conditions in which it is appropriate to behave in certain ways and in generalizing other behaviours from one setting to another.

One of the concerns about the way behavioural teaching methods have been applied is that they have failed to tackle this problem. Too often pupils have been taught specific skills in 'laboratory type' contexts (e.g. one-to-one in a quiet room), and although they may have reached their target behaviours, the skills they have learned are so unrelated to their overall curricular needs, and the context in which teaching was carried out is so rarefied, that the skills cannot be generalized to everyday life and are therefore quickly forgotten. For example it is debatable whether there is any point in teaching pupils to identify pictures of objects such as a cup, plate and spoon in a quiet room in a one-to-one teaching session when it is not time for a meal. To facilitate generalization such skills should be taught with real objects (not pictures) and at a meal time when the pupil is more likely to learn how they are used.

It is vitally important, therefore, for teaching programmes to be planned and implemented so as to maximize the likelihood that pupils will learn to generalize their skills and knowledge and discriminate between the appropriate settings in which this should be applied.

Stages of learning

The teaching techniques that have been featured so far in this and the previous chapter are primarily concerned with teaching pupils with learning difficulties to learn new skills and knowledge. This is referred to by Haring *et al* (1981) as the acquisition stage of learning. Figure 5.1 illustrates how this stage of learning relates to the stages which all people go through when learning new skills and knowledge.

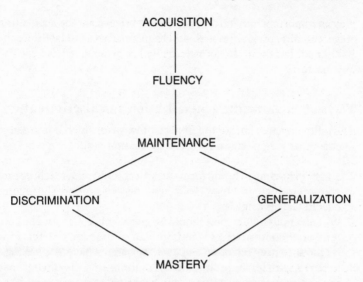

Figure 5.1: Stages of learning (Haring *et al*, 1981)

At the acquisition stage people need the maximum help. Teaching needs to be more structured and is likely to take place on a one-to-one basis or in small groups. At this stage the task itself may hold no intrinsic interest and therefore extrinsic rewards may be required. As the task is difficult for the learner, a great deal of prompting may also be needed. At the fluency stage people may be able to do the task but this is not an automatic process and they may still take a long time to complete it. To reach the maintenance stage people have not only learned the task and are fluent at it, but they also remember how to do it after a long break. However, as discussed above, it is no use remembering how to complete a task unless it is used in appropriate settings – this is the generalization and discrimination stage. Only when this has been achieved can the task be said to have been mastered.

It is helpful to refer to the learning hierarchy when planning individual programmes for pupils with learning difficulties. When planning to teach a pupil something new, that is when he/she is at the acquisition stage of learning, it is likely that teachers will need to use the techniques covered so far in this and the previous chapter, probably in a small group or on a one-to-one basis. As the pupil becomes proficient, it will not be so necessary to provide the structured input associated with these techniques and it will be important for the pupil to practise the skill in larger groups, with different people, and in different settings. Interactive teaching methods (see below) may play an important part at this stage. However, even at the acquisition stage, teaching programmes should be planned so as to facilitate the likelihood that the skills/knowledge will be generalized and eventually mastered.

Ways of encouraging generalization and discrimination

The following are some of the important ways in which it is possible to encourage generalization and discrimination.

1. Target behaviours should form part of a co-ordinated teaching programme which is broad, balanced and relevant to the pupil's overall learning needs.
2. Wherever possible pupils should be given a choice about the content of their overall programme plan and about the teaching methods to use. Too often teachers and parents have 'done things' to pupils with learning difficulties, assuming that they do not have the ability to take an active part in choosing what they would like to learn and how they should be taught.
3. Pupils should be taught in the context where they are likely to use the skill being taught. Haring *et al* (1988) consider this to be one of the keys to successful generalization. However, as mentioned in Chapter 3, it is not always easy to teach skills in context. Sometimes, in order to allow the pupil opportunities for repeated practice, it may be necessary to teach a task in a quiet room 'out of context' so that the pupil can reach the acquisition and fluency stage of learning. However, it will be vitally important for this skill to be practised in the appropriate context as well.
4. If possible more than one member of staff should be involved in teaching all aspects of the pupil's programme, as well as the parents.
5. When teaching specific target behaviours, the materials should be varied. For example, if number recognition is being taught, it is better to use numbers written in different ways, on different material, as well as plastic/wooden numbers. The same could be said when teaching early reading skills.

DEVELOPING EFFECTIVE GROUP WORK

The teaching techniques discussed so far in this and the previous chapter can be applied in individual and group teaching. However, in the past the bulk of the literature has focused on the application of these approaches to individual teaching. There has been an assumption that, because of the severity of the learning problems, pupils with learning difficulties could only learn in a one-to-one teaching session. Activities they were given when they were not receiving this intensive support were sometimes referred to as 'holding' activities as if their only purpose was to keep the pupils occupied while they were waiting to do their 'real' work with the teacher in a one-to-one session. Although one-to-one teaching will always be central to the overall educational plan for all pupils with severe learning difficulties, particularly at the acquisition stage of learning, it is clearly important to plan for effective group work as well. For one thing, even in the most generously staffed schools for pupils with severe learning difficulties, it is unlikely that a pupil will receive more than a total of half an hour's individual teaching per day and even this amount may be an overestimate. We have to plan for pupils to get maximum benefit from all their activities whether taught one-to-one or in a group.

Clearly, we have now reached the stage where the importance of planning high quality group and individual work is vital to ensure that pupils receive their entitlement to a broad, balanced and relevant curriculum. Group work in particular is essential for students to develop interpersonal and social skills in addition to providing them with opportunities to generalize skills they have learned in the more structured individual sessions.

There are now several publications (e.g. Sebba and Byers, 1992; Sebba *et al*, 1995; Smith 1991; Fagg *et al*, 1990), which have given a welcome emphasis on the need to make better use of group work with pupils with learning difficulties in a whole range of curriculum areas. In the remainder of this section we shall consider different ways in which this can be done drawing, in particular, on the work of Sebba *et al* (1995) and Byers and Rose (1996).

First of all it is important to distinguish between 'grouping' and 'group work'. Sebba *et al* (*op. cit.*) make the point that when pupils are described as working in groups they are often seated round the same table but working individually on their own separate tasks. In this kind of arrangement very little 'group work' is actually taking place in that the pupils are not working on a shared activity and interacting with each other. Simply placing pupils round the same table will not ensure that they work together. Indeed they may be getting the worst of all worlds, little attention from the teacher and no opportunities to learn from and with their peers.

However, the task of promoting effective group work is not an easy one. Sebba *et al* quote the work of Slavin (1987) who suggests that, for group work to be effective, each member has to have a part to play in working on an activity and that they should perform their part adequately. The role that each group member has should be challenging

– i.e. not too easy or too difficult, and the group as a whole should be rewarded for their success in achieving their group objective.

To do this effectively requires careful planning. In particular the size and composition of the group should be appropriate for the task they will be engaged in. The role each group member has in working on the task should be carefully negotiated and differentiated so that each has an opportunity to work at an aspect of it which is at their ability level and to play a valued part in leading to its completion.

Sebba *et al (op. cit.)* provide an interesting example of how this can be done when pupils are working in pairs, which they describe as 'an initial step towards group work'. They show how it was possible for two pupils to share in the task of drawing a picture as a record of their visit to a local agricultural college. One drew the animals they had seen and the other labelled them. They then discussed where each of the labels should be placed. Although the pupils were of different ability levels, they could still work constructively together.

Rose (1991) has used 'jigsawing' as a method of planning and implementing group work activities. This involves a detailed task analysis in which the components of an activity are interdependent. Pupils with different needs and abilities are assigned to an appropriate task, the completion of which is essential for the whole activity to be executed. In this way the work of each individual member of the group is integral to overall achievement of the activity. Sebba *et al (op. cit.)* consider that 'jigsawing' is particularly useful for practical activities such as art and craft, cookery and science. However it requires detailed planning in order to ensure that the task has been analysed accurately and that group members are assigned to the appropriate components of it.

From this brief illustration of some ways of developing effective group work skills, it can be seen that this is by no means an easy task. Teachers have to plan meticulously, while at the same time encourage pupils to work on activities which may be unfamiliar to them and to help them to develop confidence in themselves so that they can cope with the inevitable failures which will occur. They need to help pupils to see how they can learn from their mistakes as well as their successes. Effective group work often requires teachers to be extremely flexible in the way they interact with the pupils. Sometimes they will direct an activity or part of it but more often they will take on the role of facilitator and enabler so that the pupils can be given the opportunity to learn for themselves.

Some of the literature on group work seems to assume that the structured techniques, such as those discussed earlier in this chapter, are not necessary when pupils are working in groups. The stress is on the teacher as enabler and facilitator. Important though this is, teachers when managing group work still need to use techniques discussed in this and the previous chapter, for example prompting, reinforcement and task analysis.

INTERACTIVE TEACHING

Many of teaching techniques which are commonly used in group and individual teaching could also be termed 'interactive'. Interest in interactive approaches to teaching pupils with learning difficulties developed in the late 1980s (see Smith 1988, 1991). More recently Nind and Hewett (1994) have provided a full account of how the approach can be used to develop communication skills with people with severe learning disabilities.

The theoretical basis of interactive teaching lies in cognitive psychology, particularly work on parent-child interaction in the first few years of life (Schaffer, 1977; Bruner, 1975). During this period children actively participate in their own learning and through this they influence the behaviour of others and do not learn simply by being passive recipients of adult instruction. In interactive teaching the aim is to mirror methods which are used in normal parent-child interaction when working with pupils with learning difficulties and hence capitalize on the way all children learn. This 'normal' way of learning can also take place through group- and topic-based work. Running through these arguments is the assumption that, if interactive teaching works for normally developing children, then it should also work for pupils with learning difficulties.

Practical examples of the application of interactive teaching can be found in Smith (1988, 1991), Nind and Hewett (1994), Aherne *et al* (1990) and Fagg *et al* (1990a). Essentially in this approach teaching is not tightly structured but environments are created which allow for pupils to learn through spontaneous language, play and free exploration of their environment. The teacher's role is to facilitate the pupil's active interaction with the environment by picking up cues from the pupil instead of strictly directing the flow of activities. In many respects it is similar to the Gentle Teaching approach advocated by McGee *et al* (1987) and to some of the methods used in group work discussed above.

The advantages of the interactive approach are:

- That it is a 'natural' way of learning which is reflected in many schools, homes and the community.
- The absence of structure allows for more uncertainty and unpredictability over what occurs. This is in marked contrast to the

more structured behavioural approach where learning proceeds along a predetermined route. Hence, one is more likely, through interactive teaching, to arrive at unexpected but desirable outcomes.

- Interactive learning helps pupils to generalize and to experiment in how to apply their knowledge in different ways.
- Pupils learn interpersonal skills more effectively through interactive learning than through structured behavioural teaching.

Initially interactive approaches were seen in contrast to, or even incompatible with, behavioural methods. Indeed influential writers such as Nind and Hewett (1994) tend to this view. However, as is discussed in Chapter 3, the two approaches are in fact complementary and both have an important part to play in the education of all pupils including those with severe learning difficulties.

SUMMARY

In this chapter we have reviewed some of the main factors to consider when implementing teaching programmes for pupils with learning difficulties. The main points are as follows.

1. Positive reinforcement, used appropriately, makes learning effective and enjoyable.
2. Different pupils find different things rewarding, and we need to find out what is rewarding for each pupil with whom we work. We can do this by getting to know him/her well, from giving a choice of rewards or by presenting rewards one after the other.
3. Prompting is one of the major techniques that can be used to help people to learn. The three major types of prompting for teaching new tasks are physical, gestural and verbal.
4. As the pupil learns the task, prompts should be slowly withdrawn or faded. The order of fading is from greatest to least assistance (physical to gestural to verbal).
5. It is important to think carefully about the timing of prompts. Delays in prompting may result in the pupil making mistakes or becoming disheartened. Prompting too soon may deny the pupil the chance to work out how to complete the task with no help.
6. In forward training the first step is taught first and the pupil progresses forwards through the task. In backward training the order of steps is reversed and the last step is taught first, then the second to last and so on until the pupil completes the whole task unaided.
7. Backward training is recommended for teaching many tasks as

on every step the pupil completes the task and is rewarded at the natural point. However there are several tasks, e.g. learning a musical instrument, which can only be taught using forward training.

8. Pupils with learning difficulties frequently have problems in generalizing their behaviour from one setting condition to another. Conversely they may also have problems in discriminating between the setting conditions in which it is appropriate to behave in certain ways and those in which it is not.

9. In order to ensure that pupils reach the mastery stage of learning, teaching programmes should include planning for generalization and discrimination.

10. All the above techniques can be applied in group as well as in individual work. Individual work is particularly useful at the acquisition stage of learning while group work can provide opportunities for pupils to generalize their skills learned in individual sessions.

11. Effective group work requires careful planning so as to involve all pupils.

12. Interactive teaching approaches encourage pupils to control their own learning.

13. Both group work and interactive teaching are vital for the development of social and interpersonal skills.

CONCLUSION TO CHAPTERS 4 AND 5

These two chapters have covered some of the essential teaching techniques which will help in the planning and implementation of successful teaching programmes for pupils with learning difficulties. Much of the content has its theoretical roots in behavioural psychology and draws on the units of Education of the Developmentally Young (EDY) course. We have focused on methods of teaching skills and knowledge at the acquisition and fluency stage of learning although we have also considered ways of helping pupils learn to discriminate and generalize. These methods are likely to be conducted on a one-to-one or small group basis, although, as we have seen, all the techniques can also be used in larger groups and they are complementary to interactive approaches.

However it is important to remember that, to be effective, these techniques should be integrated into an overall programme plan for pupils with learning difficulties. There are therefore additional aspects not covered in these chapters which need to be considered for teaching to be successful. Two of these are referred to below.

The curriculum

We stressed in Chapter 3 that the first priority when teaching pupils with learning difficulties is to plan a programme which is broad, balanced and relevant and aimed at meeting their long-term needs to live as fulfilled and independent a life in the community as possible. Therefore the whole school curriculum should be designed with this aim in mind. Having a carefully planned and relevant curriculum should be the first priority for a school. The techniques featured in these two chapters will help in planning to teach the curriculum effectively. (See Chapter 6 for a full discussion of curriculum issues.)

Classroom management

It is impossible to implement teaching programmes effectively unless the classroom is carefully managed so that all pupils are working on useful and relevant areas from the curriculum and that staff roles have been allocated in advance. Successful classroom management is therefore one of the keys to all learning. (See Chapter 7 for a discussion of the implementation of classroom management techniques.)

CHAPTER 6

Developing the curriculum for pupils with learning difficulties

INTRODUCTION

The previous two chapters have reviewed approaches to planning and teaching pupils with learning difficulties. Essentially they are 'How to teach' chapters. In this chapter we shall focus on questions concerning 'What to teach' – the curriculum – although, as we shall see, it is not always possible to distinguish between the 'How' and 'What' of teaching.

The curriculum forms the cornerstone of successful education for all pupils, including those with SEN. Without a coherent curriculum which is relevant to the needs of pupils for whom it was designed, the quality of education will suffer. Teaching techniques and approaches discussed in the previous two chapters cannot be taught in a vacuum. They should be used to help teachers and parents to teach useful and relevant skills and knowledge which will prepare pupils for adulthood. Therefore the first priority when planning teaching programmes for a pupil or group of pupils is to decide what they should be taught. Only then should one consider the appropriate teaching methods to use.

Special schools for pupils with learning difficulties have a long history of developing innovative and imaginative curricula (see, for example, Rectory Paddock Staff, 1983; Burman *et al*, 1983). This process was further enhanced, albeit somewhat controversially, with the arrival of the National Curriculum. Indeed in the last seven years there has been a plethora of publications on curriculum development culminating in the recent book edited by Carpenter *et al* (1996).

The aim of this chapter is to provide an overview of developments in curriculum planning for pupils with learning difficulties. It is divided into three sections. In the first we consider approaches to curriculum development for pupils with learning difficulties which were popular in the 1980s, in particular developmental and objectives-based curricula. The second section discusses the impact of the

National Curriculum on current policy and practice, and the third reviews the debate about age appropriateness and the curriculum. There is insufficient space in this volume to provide a comprehensive analysis of these issues. Readers are referred to Carpenter *et al* (*op. cit.*), Coupe-O'Kane and Goldbart (1996), Byers and Rose (1996) and to recent publications from NFER and SCAA (NFER, 1995, SCAA, 1996) for a more in-depth review and discussion of current developments in the curriculum for pupils with learning difficulties.

DEVELOPMENTAL AND OBJECTIVES-BASED CURRICULA

Developmental curricula

Essentially a developmental curriculum is one in which the content follows normal developmental progression of all children. Often they are linked to developmental assessment charts, as in the Portage Checklist discussed in Chapter 2. This checklist is in fact a developmental curriculum with the implication being that children progress through the stages in the same way that a child without disabilities would do. The only difference is the assumption that the vast majority of pupils with learning difficulties need to be taught the steps of the curriculum whereas other children usually acquire them without being directly taught. Hence the Portage materials include teaching or activity cards to correspond with each item on the chart and these are designed to help parents to teach each step of the curriculum to their child. Usually the end-point of developmental curriculum corresponds with a 'mental' age level of between five and six years. According to Ware (1994) many SLD schools have been using developmental curricula for some years and she refers to documents produced by the National Curriculum Council (1993) and the DES/Welsh Office (1985) which support this view.

Ware (*op. cit.*) suggests that developmental curricula are based on the assumption that *all* pupils proceed through the same stages of development and that the progress made by pupils with learning difficulties is simply delayed. However it does not necessarily follow that these pupils learn most effectively if they are taken through the same path as their 'normal' peers (Kiernan, 1985). Moreover a developmental curriculum may not be functional for older pupils with learning difficulties who are being asked to learn skills and knowledge normally acquired by pre-school children. For example is it appropriate to teach a 15-year-old pupil with severe learning difficulties to pretend to feed a doll, a stage of play associated with a developmental level of around two years? There may be areas, not included on a developmental curriculum, which it would be extremely relevant to teach such a pupil, for example how to catch a bus or order a meal at a restaurant. These and similar items are unlikely to be found on a developmental curriculum. Finally, the fact that developmental curricula only contain items up to a developmental level of around six years can result in there being a lowering of expectations on what such pupils can achieve, with the result that people may interact with them as if they actually are a pre-school child. We will return to this point later in the chapter when we discuss issues surrounding age-appropriate teaching.

Objectives-based curricula

In the 1980s many special schools developed what came to be known as 'Objectives-based' or sometimes 'Functional' curricula. There are two broad principles underlying this approach to curriculum development. First, unlike developmental curricula, the starting-point is the skills and knowledge which pupils might have acquired by the time they leave school. Second, it is assumed that each area of the curriculum can be broken down into a hierarchically ordered sequence of behavioural objectives. Gardner *et al* (1985) provide a clear exposition of the steps which a school should follow when planning to develop an objectives-based curriculum. These are summarized as follows.

Step 1   Decide on the core areas of the curriculum.
Step 2   Decide on the components which make up each of these core areas.
Step 3   Decide on the target behaviour for each component; i.e. the final level of skill or knowledge which should be learned in order for the pupils to demonstrate that each component has been mastered.
Step 4   Break each component down into a hierarchically ordered sequence of behavioural objectives.

The actual core areas and their components varied from school to school and reflected the view of the staff on how to conceptualize their curriculum. Some included 'traditional' core areas such as functional numeracy and literacy, life and social skills each being divided into different components. Others included more general core areas such as 'knowing myself' and 'communication' – again each one being subdivided into different components.

There was also great variation in the extent to which the sequences of objectives were finely graded. Some schools worked extremely hard at producing long lists of behavioural objectives, sometimes with additional task analyses for each objective. Other schools tended to leave more gaps between the objectives and expected teachers to work out their own task analysis which would meet the needs of the particular pupil they were teaching. The more steps there were, the larger the curriculum document.

There is clearly an overlap between an objectives-based and a developmental curriculum as the further down the hierarchy one goes in an objectives curriculum, the chances are that items will match those on a developmental curriculum. They may also be written as behavioural objectives on both types of curricula. The main difference is in orientation with the developmental curriculum starting from birth while the objectives curriculum starts from the end point of the teaching process. This means that on an objectives-based curriculum it is always possible to see what the long-term goal is and how this is linked to the current teaching programme. There are also no age levels attached teaching targets on an objectives-based curriculum.

Burman *et al* (1983) discuss some of the strengths and weaknesses of objectives-based curricula. They stress the fact that they take a great deal of time to write, that all staff, other relevant agencies and parents should be involved in writing them and that, once written, they need to be continually revised as curriculum development should be seen as a dynamic process involving constant change and evolution.

The theoretical rationale underpinning the development of objectives-based curricula lies in behavioural psychology, in particular the emphasis on writing clear teaching targets as behavioural objectives and on the task analysis of teaching components. Other features of the behavioural approach, for example setting clear criteria of success for each teaching target, may also be evident.

Objectives-based curricula have brought many benefits to the education of pupils with learning difficulties. In particular the presence of a coherent curriculum document has helped schools to develop a sense of purpose and direction in that the staff know where they are going and the whole educational process is placed in context. Furthermore the fact that all staff collaborate in developing the curriculum helps them to work as a team and to feel they have ownership of what they teach. This process of curriculum development therefore represents a bottom up approach to the management of change, which, although more time consuming, usually leads to long-term benefits. The clarity of the curriculum also makes the process of education extremely accountable as it is possible to see immediately how much progress each pupil is making.

Despite the popularity of objectives-based curricula in the 1980s, they, and the way they have been implemented in some schools, have come in for considerable criticism in the last few years (see for example Billinge, 1988; Tilstone, 1991; Sebba *et al*, 1995; Nind and Hewett, 1994; Byers, 1994). Many of these authors also link criticisms of objective approaches to curriculum planning to concerns about the behavioural approach in general. In particular they argue that this approach can disempower pupils and that they become passive learners. They also express concern that objectives curricula are frequently too narrow in the subject areas covered and often exclude areas of the curriculum which are relevant to the children but which did not lend themselves to being broken down into behavioural objectives, for example co-operative play and other social interaction skills. In addition they consider that behavioural approaches overstress the value of one-to-one teaching and play down the importance of group work and of teaching pupils in natural contexts. As these arguments have been discussed more fully in Chapter 3 they will not be reviewed again here.

Despite these important concerns about the relevance of objectives curricula and behavioural methods generally, many of the above authors (e.g. Sebba *et al*, 1995, Byers, *op. cit.*) and others who have also expressed concerns about behavioural teaching (e.g. Smith, 1994; Coupe-O'Kane and Baker, 1993; the National Curriculum Council, NCC, 1992) have all stated that behavioural methods have an important part to play in planning and delivering many aspects of the curriculum. In particular they stress the relevance of behavioural objectives to teaching skills-based areas of the curriculum, for example self-help and independence activities.

THE IMPACT OF THE NATIONAL CURRICULUM ON CURRICULUM DEVELOPMENT FOR PUPILS WITH LEARNING DIFFICULTIES

Judging by the sheer volume of publications which have emerged in the last six years it would appear that the National Curriculum has had a major impact on policy and practice in curriculum development for pupils with severe learning difficulties. These include the thirteen publications in the Entitlement for All series published by David Fulton, each of which has taken a different area of the curriculum and looked at issues such as planning, strategies, assessment and recording pupil progress within the framework of the National Curriculum. In the early 1990s Ashdown *et al* (1991) edited an extremely influential book which has considered different ways in which the National Curriculum can be applied to pupils with learning difficulties. The National Curriculum Development Team (SLD) at the

University of Cambridge have produced several publications (see for example, Sebba and Clarke, 1991; Sebba and Byers, 1992; Sebba *et al*, 1995) and they were also responsible for developing Curriculum Guidance 9 on the National Curriculum for pupils with severe learning difficulties (NCC, 1992). Members of the Cambridge Team have also published further volumes on curriculum development for pupils with learning difficulties which illustrate the impact of the National Curriculum in this area (Rose *et al*, 1995; Byers and Rose, 1996). Finally an up-to-date review of approaches to delivering the curriculum to pupils with moderate to profound learning difficulties within the context of the National Curriculum has recently been published (Carpenter *et al*, 1996).

The uninitiated amongst us might be forgiven for expressing some surprise when being told that the National Curriculum is of relevance to pupils with learning difficulties, especially those with SLD and PMLD. After all, these pupils have, by definition, major problems in learning. Many will never be able to live independently in the community, get married or find employment and they may need to be supported throughout their lives. Pupils with PMLD may never be able to communicate their basic needs, they may have other physical and sensory disabilities and they may always be dependent on others in order to cope with daily living skills such as getting dressed, eating, going to the toilet. How can the National Curriculum be relevant for them? To answer this question it is necessary to say something about the context in which the National Curriculum was developed.

The National Curriculum was introduced as part of the 1988 Education Act. For many years before then many educationalists had been expressing concern that the UK was one of the few countries in the world without a National Curriculum. On the whole, therefore, all political parties and teachers' organizations were in favour of developing one.

Despite the broad range of support for the concept of a National Curriculum, the way it, and the associated testing arrangements, were introduced have caused major problems throughout the whole of the education system. These problems have been documented elsewhere and, by and large, do not affect the education of pupils with learning difficulties. Essentially the working groups charged with developing the curriculum were given an impossible time-scale in which to complete their work. As a result many curriculum documents were produced far too quickly and none were piloted systematically over a period of time. Consequently teachers, particularly in primary schools, found it impossible to implement the new curriculum. The assessment procedures were also too time-consuming and cumbersome to administer and, initially, teachers refused to have anything to do with them. As a result of the National Curriculum's somewhat traumatic introduction, the government have allowed it to be slimmed down considerably and the assessment arrangements have been simplified, being based more on pencil-and-paper tests.

As far as pupils with learning difficulties were concerned, the authors of the curriculum documents for each of the core and foundation subjects appeared to assume that such pupils would need a separate curriculum and that they would therefore be excluded or 'disapplied' from it. The notion that certain pupils should be excluded from the National Curriculum caused consternation among those working in the special needs field. It implied that pupils with SEN were being segregated from the mainstream. This was manifestly contrary to current developments towards more integrated and inclusive education for these children. If one of the goals of special education is the inclusion of pupils with SEN within a mainstream context, it was imperative for all these children to be included in the National Curriculum and its associated assessment procedures. If this did not happen there was a danger of a return to a two-track system of education, with special and mainstream schools being seen as completely separate from each other.

For pupils with learning difficulties this dilemma caused something of a hiatus among professionals and academics working in this area. After all, as we have suggested, special schools had been at the forefront of developing innovative curricula throughout the 1980s. Indeed a case could be made for suggesting that these schools were the only educational establishments who had carefully developed interesting, functional and relevant curricula for their pupils. This process had also brought staff together who felt they had ownership of the curriculum and were committed to making it work. All of a sudden a hastily developed and wholly inadequate National Curriculum was introduced into mainstream schools. In order to avoid the risk of being excluded from mainstream education, special schools were being asked to abandon their own carefully developed curricula and to take on board this new curriculum which had not been developed for children with SEN in any case. To maintain a separate curriculum would reinforce the impression that special education was, and would always be, segregated from the mainstream sector. Therefore the reason for including pupils with SEN in the National Curriculum had nothing to do with its quality. (In fact as we have seen, mainstream teachers were extremely hostile to many parts of it.) Pupils should be included *solely* because mainstream children had to be subjected to it. The fact that what was on offer in special schools may have been far better was an irrelevant consideration!

Ware (1994a) encapsulates this difficulty when she states that 'there is a real danger that the National Curriculum could replace previous good practice'. Similar concerns have been expressed by others (see for example Cornell and Carden, 1990; and Emblem and Conti-Ramsden, 1990).

This problem can be highlighted with reference to the following analogy. Imagine a housing estate containing gardens of different shapes and sizes. The occupants of the houses shared in the responsibility for tending to the gardens. Each garden had its individual characteristics but there were similarities between many of them, particularly the larger ones. The occupants of one of the houses had taken particular care over their garden. All members of the family had worked collaboratively together and were continuing to do so since there were always ways of improving the garden. To all those living elsewhere in the housing estate, this particular garden looked extremely well cared for and especially suited to those living and working in the house. The expertise and commitment of all involved in its creation was universally acknowledged. One day, however, things changed. The local authority decided that all the other gardens in the housing estate would be improved if they were covered in concrete, and within a very short space of time this dramatic change took place. People in the well-tended garden now felt uneasy. If everyone else wants their garden to be covered in concrete, shouldn't we do the same? After all we now look very different and separate and surely our ultimate aim is to be included in the whole community. Consequently we should have some of that concrete too!

This analogy illustrates the problems faced by schools for pupils with learning difficulties following the introduction of the National Curriculum. Should these schools abandon their curricula and teach the core and foundation subjects of the new curriculum? Could their existing curriculum be adapted in order to make this possible? One response to the problem of integrating the National Curriculum with a school's curriculum for pupils with learning difficulties was to view the attainment targets and statements of attainments as objectives to be task-analysed. They could therefore be broken down into very small steps that could be taught to pupils with learning difficulties. In this way these pupils would have access to the National Curriculum as it would be possible to see how the objectives on the IEP were linked to it. There are two main problems with this approach. First, the sheer number of steps that are needed to break down statements of attainment to the level appropriate for pupils with learning difficulties is extremely large. For example the resulting IEP might include objectives such as making eye contact or reaching for toys. These could conceivably be seen as part of the English or Science

National Curriculum but the gap between what the pupils are work-ing on and the content of the English curriculum is so great that to call these activities a part of the National Curriculum is pure tokenism. Second, pupils with SLD need to learn many basic skills, particularly in the self-help area – e.g. feeding and dressing, which are not and could never be included in the National Curriculum no mat-ter how it is task-analysed. Therefore, for some pupils, their IEPs could not be related to the National Curriculum.

These approaches to incorporating the National Curriculum for pupils with learning difficulties have been criticized as being inap-propriate by Sebba *et al* (1995). As an alternative her team of researchers at Cambridge and the Manchester Teacher Fellows, who gave birth to the Entitlement for All series mentioned above, adopt-ed a different strategy. They focused more on the National Curriculum programmes of study as a starting-point for rethinking curricula for pupils with SLD. Much of their work was also influ-enced by concerns about the rigidity of objectives models of curriculum development and by their reservations about the appro-priateness of behavioural methods in general. It was as if the National Curriculum provided an impetus for a much-needed review of cur-riculum development for all pupils with learning difficulties.

Although, as we have seen in Chapter 3, some of these concerns about behavioural methods may have been misguided, many innova-tive approaches to curriculum development have emerged from the Cambridge and Manchester Teams and from several other authors (see for example Ashdown *et al*, 1991; Coupe-O'Kane and Baker, 1993; Rose *et al*, 1994). In particular these writers have provided examples of how to teach IEPs through cross-curricular themes, how to develop effective group work, how to ensure that teaching takes place in meaningful contexts and how to empower pupils by teaching them to take an active part in choosing what they do.

The advent of the National Curriculum has therefore given cur-riculum development for pupils with SLD a shot in the arm. The legal entitlement for all pupils to have a broad, balanced and relevant cur-riculum which should facilitate maximum access to mainstream provision is an overarching principle which has been universally accepted. However it is also accepted that, for many pupils with severe learning difficulties, their detailed educational programmes could never resemble the content of the National Curriculum in any way. Jordan and Powell (1994) reflect this opinion when they refer to 'Curriculum Principles for All' as opposed to a 'National Curriculum for All'. Norwich (1992) takes a similar view when he states that the National Curriculum should be seen as an entitlement to a common curriculum framework.

Given the sheer volume of publications on the National Curriculum and the education of pupils with learning difficulties one would expect it to have had widespread impact on current practice. However, such evidence as there is suggests that this impact has been patchy, to say the least. Heggie (1994) for example has been involved in a project which examined working practices in LEAs and special schools. She concludes that the National Curriculum 'is simply not of much relevance to pupils who are functioning at an extremely early level of development'. However her own school has incorporated aspects of the National Curriculum 'where relevant and appropriate'. Humphreys (1995) offers a frank account of a one-day conference on the relevance of the National Curriculum for pupils with SLD held in June 1995 at which representatives of SCAA, OFSTED and NFER were among the main speakers. According to him almost all of the 150 teachers present did not share the views expressed by the majority of the main speakers who felt that the National Curriculum was relevant for this group of pupils. These teachers felt that using existing guidelines and documentation to incorporate the National Curriculum was 'tokenistic, reductionist and at times, naive'. Humphreys goes on to say that 'many did not appreciate how the needs of their pupils could be entirely met within the National Curriculum'. 'Some of the examples of good practice we have been given have been very helpful but, frankly some of them have been absolutely daft!' Humphreys concludes with a plea for a 'national professional debate, as well as more practical guidance, that significantly exceeds the current biased perspective'. Halpin and Lewis (1996), in a survey of twelve special school headteachers, eight of whom managed schools for pupils with learning difficulties, conclude that 'in various ways the National Curriculum is interpreted as either irrelevant to the special school context or is accepted at the level of rhetoric while making minimal impact'.

It may be the case that those who are sceptical about the relevance of the National Curriculum have adopted too literal a view as to how it might be implemented for pupils with learning difficulties. The documents developed by the Cambridge team and the Entitlement for All series, for example, take a more balanced view of the relevance of the National Curriculum and contain extremely helpful guidance on all aspects of the curriculum. These should be extremely useful to schools which are engaged on the ongoing process of curriculum development.

We conclude this section with reference to recent publications on curriculum development for pupils with learning difficulties, especially the books by Byers and Rose (1996), Carpenter *et al* (1996),

NFER (1995) and SCAA (1996). The book edited by Carpenter and his colleagues, in particular, contains a number of interesting chapters on implementing specific aspects of the curriculum in addition to some overall contributions on the process of curriculum development, assessment and self-advocacy. The introductory chapter by Carpenter and Ashdown (1996) summarizes key points from the SCAA (1996) guidance:

- there is an entitlement to a whole curriculum, not just the National Curriculum;
- not all individual priorities can be met through the National Curriculum;
- tokenism should not be tolerated and there must be a meaningful involvement in subject-focused activities;
- teaching priorities may be related to cross-curricular skills such as communication, personal and social development, information technology capability, and the cross-curricular process of investigation and problem-solving;
- unavoidable routines and care procedures should not be viewed as interruptions to teaching but as valuable teaching opportunities that should not be rushed and should be planned carefully;
- teachers should not be anxious to count the hours and minutes allocated to each subject of the National Curriculum, although there is still need for a rigorous planning of the curriculum;
- breadth and balance in the curriculum is something to be achieved over a year in a key stage rather than a week or half term.

(adapted from Carpenter and Ashdown, 1996, pp. 4–5)

Although the guidance from SCAA is intended for pupils with PMLD, the principles behind them apply to all pupils with learning difficulties. The guidance makes it clear that, far from imposing restrictions on curriculum development for pupils with learning difficulties, the National Curriculum should help schools to develop appropriate curricula to meet the needs of the pupils for whom it caters. Indeed SCAA (1996) suggests the following six-phase systematic approach to planning the curriculum:

Phase 1	Policy-making.
Phase 2	Developing schemes of work/long-term planning.
Phase 3	Developing schemes of work/medium-term planning.
Phase 4	Developing schemes of work/short-term planning.
Phase 5	Assessment and recording.
Phase 6	Review and evaluation.

This six-phase approach is discussed in some detail by Ashdown (1996). Essentially it represents a model which begins with broad statements of aims, policies and priorities which are progressively narrowed down to include termly sequences of work for class groups and then to individual programmes of work. The implementation of the curriculum should be informed by the school's assessment and recording system and by regular reviews and evaluations. In implementing the curriculum, teachers need to plan IEPs which include short- and long-term targets and suggestions as to how these should be taught and recorded. It also recommends that, when planning, assessing and reporting on the progress made by pupils with PMLD, teachers should distinguish between activities which are 'experienced' and those which are 'achieved'. The six-phase approach to planning the curriculum includes guidance on teaching methods and classroom organization and management, reflecting a point made at the beginning of this chapter that it is not always possible or even desirable to separate teaching methods from content.

In his chapter Ashdown (1996) suggests that curriculum development for pupils with learning difficulties should be an ongoing process involving all staff, preferably co-ordinated by a member of the senior management team. To this extent he is encouraging schools to continue the innovative work on curriculum development which, as we have seen, has been a feature of special education since the early 1980s.

CAN THE CURRICULUM FOR PUPILS WITH LEARNING DIFFICULTIES BE AGE-APPROPRIATE?

A further controversial area in planning what to teach pupils with learning difficulties concerns the extent to which it is possible or desirable for the curriculum to be age-appropriate. This debate has been highlighted recently by Nind and Hewett (1996), Porter *et al* (1996) and Smith (1996). Porter and her colleagues refer to Matson *et al*'s (1993) definition of age-appropriate behaviour as that which is 'socially normative' and 'consistent with same age peers'. Put quite simply, examples of age-appropriate activities could be teaching an adolescent to travel independently by bus, to order a pint of beer in a pub, to wear make-up. These, it is assumed, are the kinds of activities which adolescents without disabilities typically engage in and therefore they should form part of the curriculum for adolescents with learning difficulties. Examples of non-age-appropriate activities might be teaching a similar adolescent to complete a jigsaw or to sing nursery rhymes. It is also argued that staff and parents should behave in an age-appropriate way with pupils with learning difficulties. For example we should not put our arm around a teenager with learning difficulties when first meeting him/her (unless they are very distressed) while such behaviour might be considered appropriate with a four-year-old. Similarly it may be appropriate to reward a four-year-old with sweets but not an adolescent.

It is important to bear in mind that the concept of age-appropriateness is socially constructed. Society, through its formal and informal structures (e.g. schools, families, governments), decides what is age-appropriate behaviour. For example the British government decrees that it is only age-appropriate to drink alcohol in a pub when one reaches the age of 18. Other governments have different laws. In some cultures it is age-appropriate for children to begin paid work before they reach puberty; in most Western societies this is only the case after the age of 16. Some families in the UK living in inner-city apartments with no gardens might consider it age-appropriate for their six-year-old child to play in the street. Other families, possibly living in houses with gardens, might consider that a six-year-old is too young to engage in this behaviour. The fact that the concept of age-appropriateness is socially constructed means that teachers, parents and pupils may disagree about what is and is not age-appropriate. This can have major implications when deciding what to teach a person with learning difficulties.

The arguments in favour of age-appropriate teaching stem from the concept of normalization or social role valorization (Wolfensberger, 1983). Some of the principles of normalization and the impact that it has had in the planning and delivery of services for people with disabilities have been referred to in the introduction to this book. As regards the debate about age-appropriateness, the arguments can be summarized as follows. All professionals and parents should interact with people with learning difficulties in a manner which promotes dignity and respect and this comes from providing a curriculum similar to other people of the same age. By treating them as younger pupils we are teaching and reinforcing inappropriate behaviour and may prevent them from making progress. Our expectations of what they might achieve could also be reduced as we may think of them as young children. In addition, by interacting with them in a non-age-appropriate way we run the risk of reinforcing the image that society might have of people with learning difficulties as being 'eternal children' (Nind and Hewett, *op. cit.*). Furthermore people with learning difficulties typically present an extremely varied profile of skills and abilities. Although some may be pre-verbal and have other associated language and physical disabilities, they will have developed normal sexual feelings not typically associated with young children. Treating such a person as a young child by, for example, getting close to and stroking him/her in an intensive interaction session may arouse inappropriate sexual feelings in the young person. Such feelings would probably not emerge if the interaction with him/her was age-appropriate.

Despite these arguments, it is difficult and not always good practice to teach age-appropriate activities to people with learning difficulties. First, the extent of the pupils' learning difficulties inevitably means that their developmental level will be very different from their chronological age. To teach them as if they were at their chronological age may deny them valuable opportunities for learning. This point is highlighted graphically by Nind and Hewett (1996) when writing about their work with pre-verbal people with very severe learning disabilities. Although they have been accused of working in a non-age-appropriate way, Nind (1996) has shown that through intensive interaction people make sustained gains in their ability to initiate social contacts and there is a reduction in ritualistic behaviour. She argues that such changes would not have occurred if their carers had interacted in an age-appropriate way.

Second, pupils with learning difficulties may enjoy working on tasks which are not age-appropriate and, given the chance, they may choose to engage in them. Giving people choice respects their independence and autonomy and, if the tasks they choose give them pleasure and do not disturb others or cause injury to anyone, and if they reduce the incidence of challenging behaviour, then it seems churlish to deny them their opportunity to make these choices. A similar point was made in Chapter 5 with respect to the use of non-age-appropriate rewards.

There are, however, examples of professionals interacting in an age-appropriate way which can be either tokenistic or extremely dangerous and distressing. In one example, known to the author, an 18-year-old young man with quite complex and severe learning disabilities, who was shortly moving into a flat, was taken by his carers to a large department store in order to choose furniture. Unfortunately this young person had major communication difficulties, he did not understand that he was moving into a flat and almost certainly did not understand that people could buy things from shops. Therefore, although he may have learned something from his trip to the department store, he certainly took no meaningful part in choosing the furniture. In a second example, referred to by Farrell (1995), a young man in his twenties with learning difficulties was being taken home by his carer at the end of the day. At one point on the journey he informed his carer that he would now make his own way home. The carer, respecting the young person's right to choose, said goodbye and left him to go home by himself. Unfortunately the young man did not know the way home and hours later he was discovered by his anxious and distressed mother wandering around a shopping centre.

From the above discussion it can be seen that the age-appropriate debate is complex and that there are no easy answers. Clearly, many pupils with learning difficulties are likely to be functioning at a developmental level far behind their chronological age. Teachers and parents have a responsibility to help them to develop and this may inevitably mean that they will be taught activities which are aimed at people much younger than them. Porter *et al* (1996) argue that although a developmental and functional (objectives) curriculum are by no means incompatible and may include very similar items, the 'contexts for teaching' are different. A developmental curriculum is more related to young children's developmental sequences whereas a functional curriculum is focused on skills for independent living. Therefore, although we may teach children activities that may seem to be non-age appropriate, if we use a functional curriculum, we can at least see how such activities link to more age-appropriate tasks, even if the pupil is a long way from learning them. This may sound tokenistic but at least the learning process is placed within an 'age-appropriate' conceptual framework.

Perhaps there are other aspects of the age-appropriate debate which are less controversial. For example adolescents with learning difficulties should dress like teenagers (e.g. girls should not wear pigtails, boys should not wear shorts). Young people, including those with PMLD, should not be denied opportunities to visit restaurants, cinemas and theatres etc. Wherever possible we should involve them in making choices in how they run their lives. Not only is this age-appropriate, but it is also good education.

Like many aspects of the education of children with SLD it is important to maintain a balanced view in the age-appropriate debate. It is clearly not feasible to teach age-appropriate activities all the time, and, as Nind and Hewett illustrate, adults with the most severe disabilities can make progress through intensive interaction sessions with their carers. However it would probably not be appropriate to engage in intensive interaction at all times of the day. People also need opportunities to engage in more age-appropriate activities such as watching television or going out shopping. If these opportunities are denied to them, we may be underestimating their abilities and run the risk of assuming that they will never learn from engaging in everyday tasks.

We should also encourage people to make choices. However, if the choices they make are inappropriate, teachers and parents should find ways of teaching them to choose alternative activities. Porter *et al* (1996) provide an excellent illustration of teachers attempting to achieve this with a 17-year-old young man who had profound learning difficulties and some 'autistic' behaviours. When given the chance he chose to play with one specific musical box designed for use with young children and became quite distressed if this was removed from him. Through gradually encouraging him to undertake other tasks, for example searching for the musical box in different containers and by introducing other types of music, it was hoped that he could become less reliant on the musical box.

Smith (1996) concludes her discussion of the debate by suggesting that less emphasis should be placed on what is 'age-appropriate or developmentally appropriate' and that we should concentrate on the process through which each person is enabled to interact with his or her environment, to control aspects of that environment, and, above all to experience the satisfaction, self-esteem and stimulus to further development which comes with such achievements. Age-appropriate activities and developmentally-appropriate activities are not prescriptions, but they can be means to that end.

CONCLUSION

The following is a summary of the key points which have emerged from this chapter on curriculum development for pupils with learning difficulties.

1. Pupils with learning difficulties should have access to a broad, balanced and relevant curriculum in line with the requirements of the National Curriculum.
2. This curriculum should incorporate carefully planned and implemented programmes of individual and group work.
3. Curriculum development for all pupils with learning difficulties should be an ongoing and dynamic process with all teachers having an important part to play in shaping the curriculum in their own school. Indeed this has always been one of the main strengths of curriculum development in special education.
4. Finally the curriculum should reflect the overall aims of education: that of enabling pupils with learning difficulties to develop skills and knowledge which will help them to live as independently in the community as possible, to make informed choices and to make and sustain mutually beneficial relationships with others.

CHAPTER 7

Classroom management: from principles to practice

INTRODUCTION: AIMS OF CLASSROOM MANAGEMENT

A central feature of the successful education of all pupils with and without disabilities is the extent to which the learning environment (the classroom) is managed. There are countless studies which show conclusively, and not surprisingly, that ineffective classroom management adversely affects pupils' learning and standards of behaviour.

Before discussing the factors which contribute to successful classroom management, it is necessary to define what is meant by the term. In this chapter a well-managed class is defined as one in which *at all times the pupils work on a broad, balanced and relevant range of tasks/activities which are of interest to them and which are tailored to their assessed needs.*

As can be seen this definition of an effectively managed classroom is written in term of outcomes, i.e. what the end point should be when teachers manage their classroom successfully. Although it is likely that most teachers would not find this definition particularly contentious, there is considerable disagreement among them and among parents, pupils, and even OFSTED inspectors as to how to achieve the goal of successful classroom management. For example, any two successful teachers may well tolerate different noise levels or they may have individual preferences for classroom seating arrangements. Indeed it is, and should be, a feature of the diverse nature of the educational process that pupils experience a wide variety of teaching styles and approaches during their educational career all of which can lead to their classrooms being managed effectively.

Despite these differences in teaching styles it could be argued that, to achieve the goal of effective classroom management defined above, as a basic minimum all teachers should aim to:

- have assessed accurately the individual needs of each of the pupils;
- plan IEPs for each pupil which reflect these assessed needs and also cover a broad, balanced and relevant curriculum;
- ensure that the timetable is planned in such a way as to allow sufficient time for the pupils to work on their IEP;
- organize the classroom environment and seating arrangements so as to facilitate pupils' learning;
- have sufficient access to in-school and out-of-school materials, equipment and resources;
- reward pupils' efforts and achievements appropriately.

The above could be seen as an unattainable list of aspirations which are impossible to meet given the real world of the British classroom in which class sizes are too large, where the curriculum is seen to be irrelevant by many pupils and teachers, and where there is a continual squeeze on resources. However, they provide a set of aims which teachers in any educational setting should strive to achieve. The closer one gets to them, the more likely it will be that pupils will enjoy school, that they will make progress in their learning and that they will behave well.

Although the aims for classroom management are the same in any educational setting – infant, junior, secondary and special school – there are some specific factors which need to be considered when planning high-quality education for pupils with learning difficulties. These take account of the broad aims listed above but, in addition, they also reflect the nature of the special needs presented by these pupils. First, classes in special schools and units typically contain between eight and fifteen pupils. Second, the very nature of their learning difficulties means that these pupils require more direct individual teaching than their peers who do not have learning difficulties. Third, group work needs to be carefully managed in order to ensure maximum participation. Fourth, there is almost always more than one member of staff working in the classroom.

Taking these factors into account this chapter considers ways in which teachers of pupils with learning difficulties can manage their classes effectively. It is divided into the following sections: the organization of staff roles, the timetable, recording progress and classroom seating arrangements. Throughout, the emphasis is on classroom management in schools for pupils with SLD although the principles can be applied in MLD schools as well. They are also relevant to classroom management in integrated settings within mainstream schools containing pupils with learning difficulties although there are some specific issues related to the deployment of support workers in such settings which need to be considered. These are discussed in Chapter 10.

THE ORGANIZATION OF STAFF ROLES

The planned organization of staff roles is one of the cornerstones of effective classroom management for pupils with SLD. As all class-rooms contain more than one member of staff, it is important for their roles to be planned and agreed at the outset.

Early research in this area focused on working with adults with learning difficulties (Porterfield *et al*, 1977). Room Management, as it was then known, provided a means of allocating staff roles in hospital wards and special needs units of adult training centres. Essentially there was an Individual Worker who conducted individual teaching programmes, a Room Manager who kept everybody else busy and an Individual Helper who assisted the Room Manager by dealing with visitors, any emergencies and, if time allowed, worked with clients alongside the Room Manager. The duties of the Room Manager were carefully prescribed and included providing every client with something to do, rewarding those who were busy and prompting those who were not. Research evaluating the impact of Room Management, reviewed by Farrell *et al* (1992) and Ware (1994b) (see for, example, Porterfield *et al*, 1977; Coles and Blunden, 1979; Crisp and Sturmey, 1988) has shown that client engagement – i.e. their 'on task' behaviour – under Room Management conditions increased dramatically, from 31 per cent to 80 per cent in Porterfield and Blunden's study. Mansell *et al* (1982), however, found that there was a differential effect on client engagement following Room Management for clients who have more profound learning difficulties. These clients were less likely to be engaged for significant amounts of time whether or not they were in Room Management conditions.

Following the development of Room Management in adult settings, McBrien and Weightman (1980) and Thomas (1985) developed the technique for use in schools. The following scheme which portrays the various roles of staff members in Room Management is similar to the one described by Thomas (*op. cit.*). In this scheme it is assumed that there are three staff members who are allocated the following roles during the Room Management (or Activity) period.

Individual Worker: Responsible for teaching individual programmes, usually in a corner of the classroom reserved for this purpose.

Room Manager: Responsible for:

- giving each group member a choice of materials;
- quickly prompting each member to start using the materials;
- moving materials so that they are in easy reach;
- moving round the group to praise and reward group members who are busy;
- giving minimum attention (typically quick prompts) to group members who are not busy.

Mover: Responsible for dealing with interruptions or emergencies, toileting pupils and, if time, helping the Room Manager.

Studies have shown that under Room Management conditions it is possible to raise the level of engagement in pupils with SLD but less so for pupils with PMLD whose level of engagement appears to remain extremely low (around 20 per cent to 40 per cent) no matter how they are taught (Ware and Evans, 1987; McBrien and Weightman, 1980). Both these studies also found that in Room Management conditions staff divided their time more evenly across the group whereas in non-Room Management conditions more able pupils received twice as much attention than their less able peers. Finally Pope (1988) confirmed that under Room Management there was a marked decrease in pupils' inappropriate behaviour.

Room Management procedures therefore provided a structure for organizing staff roles which could be applied successfully in SLD schools. The main problem, however, was the fact that in the early development of the technique, only certain periods of the day were set aside when these procedures operated. For the rest of the day classrooms were organized as they had been before. The challenge, therefore, was to try to incorporate Room Management techniques into a co-ordinated system of classroom management throughout the school day. In this way staff roles could be carefully planned, adopting some of the principles of Room Management, and applied at all times. To do this necessitated reducing the intensity of the Room Manager's role as described above, since working in this way for long periods is completely exhausting. However, the *principles of systematically giving pupils regular attention and praise and of ensuring that they have enough to do* is one which should be applied at all times. The planned allocation of staff roles helps to ensure that this occurs.

Effective classroom management, therefore, requires staff roles to be planned and allocated throughout the whole day. This does not mean that the same tasks should always be performed by the same staff member. On the contrary, staff roles should be interchangeable.

This prevents staff from becoming bored with performing the same task all the time and it conveys the message that each and every role is equally important – individual and group work, toileting, feeding etc. Furthermore the number and range of roles that each staff member takes on varies considerably and depends on the age and ability of the students, the numbers of staff and the resources and equipment which are available. By no means is it expected that the roles should match the ones originally described by Thomas (*op. cit.*) although it is likely that for some of the day at least one staff member will be allocated to individual work.

One immediate effect of having carefully planned staff roles which have been allocated in advance is that staff know exactly what they should be doing and with whom they will be working at the start of each day. This reduces the amount of staff–staff interaction and increases the amount of time teachers interact with the pupils. How effective this is also depends to some extent on the ratio of staff to students and on the students' ability. In classes in schools for pupils with severe learning difficulties there are typically around ten students to two or three staff – usually one teacher and one or two classroom assistants who may be qualified nursery nurses. However in a class containing students with profound and multiple learning difficulties the ratio is frequently more favourable: around three staff to eight students.

It goes without saying that it is essential for staff to work well together in any team-teaching situation. If they do not get on with each other, this will adversely affect the management of the classroom. Staff may attend in-service courses on classroom management and plan meticulously but if there are problems in the working relationships between them, all this advanced planning will not be transferred into effective action. Initially this is an issue for the senior managers in a school. They need to know their staff well and make judgements as to who will work well together. Inevitably this involves them in conducting sensitive negotiations and in making difficult decisions.

THE TIMETABLE

It is a feature of all schools, special and mainstream, that there is a timetable for each class and this is an important component of successful classroom management. The wide variety of abilities and the range of complex needs among the pupils with learning difficulties is reflected in the differences between timetables for different classes. There are also constraints of time and resources which inevitably impose restrictions on what is possible to include on a timetable.

Nevertheless, when planning the timetable the following factors should be common to all classes in a school for pupils with learning difficulties:

- The timetable should show that the pupils are following a broad, balanced and relevant curricula both within and outside the classroom. Class themes, topics and related activities should also be listed.
- If pupils are working on priority targets which will be taught on a one-to-one basis, the timetable should indicate when these sessions will take place.
- The time when different group activities take place should also be stated including times when the class is working as a whole group, e.g. for music, and when small groups will be doing specific activities, e.g. working in the library.
- The timetable should indicate which activities each staff member will be engaged in.
- It should be regularly updated at planning meetings of the whole staff team.

A key factor, mentioned above, which has a major impact on the timetable concerns the number of priority targets which it is feasible or desirable to teach on a one-to-one basis at any one time. It is not likely to be productive to overload the pupil with too many 'targets' as there is only so much that pupils can take in at any one time. Furthermore the amount of one-to-one teaching which is possible depends on the numbers of staff and pupils there are in the class. However, it is suggested that, as priority targets are selected as being important for the pupil to learn, they should be taught frequently (e.g. at least three times per week). Consequently, given that there are several pupils in each class, the optimum number of targets per pupil is likely to be around four.

An example of the timetable for a nursery class in a school for pupils with SLD is given in Figure 7.1.

This class contains eighteen pupils aged between two and five years, nine of whom have severe learning difficulties and nine are 'play group' pupils. Staff numbers vary between three and four. There is one class teacher, two nursery nurses and one classroom assistant. The timetable is planned at a weekly meeting of the four staff at which time their roles are allocated. Individual teaching takes place in the morning and is restricted to the nine pupils with learning difficulties. Their progress is recorded as is the amount of individual teaching each pupil receives. Each pupil's programme also contains aims and objectives for group work and out-of-class activities. The

	MORNING				AFTERNOON	
			Lower School Music			
MON	Individual Group Room Splash Room	*Maria* *Joanne* *Doreen* *Sue*			Computer Soft Room	*Doreen* *Joanne*
TUES	Individual Group Room Computer	*Doreen* *Maria* *Michelle* *Joanne*	Individual Room Computer Soft Room	*Maria* *Michelle* *Joanne* *Doreen*	Leisure	
WED	Individual Group Room	*Joanne* *Michelle* *Doreen/Maria*	Hydrotherapy Individual Group	*Doreen/Joanne* *Jackie/Michelle* *Maria*	Home Economics Shopping	*Doreen* *Joanne/Maria*
THURS	Individual Group Room	*Joanne* *Doreen* *Maria*	Individual Library Group	*Doreen* *Maria* *Joanne*	Swimming Soft Room	*Joanne/Maria* *Doreen/Mary*
FRI	Individual Group Room Splash Room	*Maria* *Joanne* *Doreen* *Sue*	Individual Group Library Library	*Doreen* *Maria* *Joanne* *Joanne*	Group Dancing Soft Room Singing	*Maria* *Doreen* *Joanne* *Michelle*

Figure 7.1: Nursery timetable – staff roles (from McBrien *et al*, 1992)

timetable indicates how much time is devoted to out-of-class activities, e.g. music with the whole junior department, shopping and library work and when the whole group divides, as for example on Wednesday afternoon when some pupils go shopping and some work in the home economics room.

In Figure 7.1 'Individual' refers to the staff member who does individual work; 'Group' refers to the person who works with a small group on a topic; 'Room' refers to the staff member who deals with interruptions, toilets the pupils and, if time allows, helps the group worker. 'Splash' and 'Soft room' are areas in the school where pupils can engage in water play and gross motor activities respectively. In the 'leisure' afternoon the pupils throughout the junior department can choose a particular activity and may work in another class and/or with different staff.

RECORDING PUPIL PROGRESS

One important aspect of successful classroom management involves the recording of individual and group work. The whole question of how to record pupils' progress in a way which provides maximum information with minimum inconvenience for teachers has been the subject of much debate, particularly since the advent of the National Curriculum. The main aim of recording is to monitor the progress of the pupils. This helps to make the teaching process accountable and enables staff to assess the effectiveness of programmes of work for individuals and groups of pupils. This information can be used for many purposes: it is helpful in planning and adapting further teaching programmes for individuals and groups, it can form the basis of collaborative work with parents and other agencies, and it can be used as part of annual reviews and transition plans. All recording systems should be easy to use and agreed upon by staff and, if possible, parents and pupils. However they must not be too time-consuming to complete and interrupt the flow of teaching. Recording should provide information about the effectiveness of teaching and not interfere with it. Sebba *et al* (1995) suggest that there should be a whole school policy on record-keeping which is evolved following full consultation with all the staff. This may be complemented by individual teachers devising their own systems for particular individuals or situations.

There is no one effective way of recording an individual pupil's progress. As mentioned in Chapter 2, teachers continually assess the progress of their pupils on the curriculum – curriculum-based assessment – and this information informs their programme planning. Most schools have a pupil file containing information as to the progress he/she is making on the curriculum – a curriculum record. Individual programmes of work and priority teaching targets are derived from this information. Teachers may then use separate forms or cards to record the progress the pupil makes on these priority targets using a system which provides a record of how well the pupil worked in each teaching session. This may involve recording the pupil's performance on each teaching trial as well as other general comments. When the pupil achieves the target, the information is entered on the curriculum record.

As with recording individual pupil progress, there is no one way of recording group work. Some schools have a system of simply recording the activities that the pupils have worked on without indicating the progress they have made. This information is used to ensure that each pupil is getting access to the whole curriculum. In addition the activities are chosen because the pupils finds them interesting and/or because they provide opportunities for them to practise skills they are learning in individual work.

It is also possible to record the progress made by individual pupils in a group work session. Figure 7.2 provides an example of a record

Class: Playgroup								Date: 27/6/95		
Group activity: Making a tomato sandwich										
Pupils:	1	2	3	4	5	6	7	8	9	10
Name bread										
Name butter										
Name knife										
Name tomatoes										
Name salt										
Steps										
1. Butter bread										
2. Put tomato on bread										
3. Sprinkle salt										
4. Put other slice on										
5. Cut sandwich in two										

Pupils

1. Roni	6. Sonali
2. Kanta	7. Raja
3. Shanti	8. Razia
4. Abdul	9. Palbinder
5. Paro	10. Sheba

Figure 7.2: Group activity recording sheet (adapted from Farrell and Banerjee, 1996)

which can show how much progress each member of a group made when learning to make a tomato sandwich. There is con-erable variation in the abilities within the group who are working i this task and therefore they are not expected to complete all of it. The record form takes this into account. For a more complete discussion of different ways of recording group work, readers should consult Lawson (1992).

CLASSROOM SEATING ARRANGEMENTS

The seating arrangements should be such that they facilitate maximum pupil engagement in the activities they are working on. In primary eduction there has been considerable debate about the benefits of either seating pupils in rows or grouping them around tables. The current emphasis on the benefits of whole-class teaching suggests that pupils will attend better if they are in rows. However, this is contrary to a philosophy of co-operative group work, shared and discovery learning which has been a feature of primary education for many years.

As far as pupils with learning difficulties are concerned, Sebba *et al* (1995) – as we have seen in Chapter 5 – consider that placing such pupils around a table may, in fact, do nothing to encourage group work; the pupils are just grouped together. Indeed there is some evidence that, if a teacher wishes to work with a group, then horseshoe seating arrangements seem to ensure the maximum participation from the pupils (Evans, 1982; Sturmey and Crisp, 1989). Such arrangements enable the teacher to maintain eye contact and engage with the pupils.

The arrangement of all the classroom furniture should also be appropriate for the tasks the pupils are involved in. For example in the senior class, where students are likely to be focusing on learning skills for independent living, the organization of some areas of the classroom may resemble different parts of the home, e.g. the kitchen or the living room, so that the pupils can learn skills which are used in these settings. Traditional classroom seating arrangements will not be appropriate for these students.

CONCLUSION

Effective classroom management is one of the keys to successful education for pupils with learning difficulties. Not only does this ensure that teachers and pupils are engaged to the fullest extent on activities that are of interest and relevance to them and at their ability level, but it also results in the reduction of the incidence of challenging behaviour (Pope, 1988). Indeed, as discussed in Chapter 8, successful classroom management is a key strategy in the prevention of challenging behaviour. This chapter has briefly reviewed some of the factors leading to the development of effective classroom management schemes.

Perhaps the most important feature of classroom management in the education of pupils with learning difficulties is the planned allocation of staff roles. Although these are interchangeable and all staff may undertake the full range of duties over a period of time, the class teacher has the responsibility for planning and managing the class, for drawing up the timetable and, in collaboration with other staff, for devising the recording systems. Although the 'fly on the wall' of a class containing pupils with learning difficulties may not be able to determine who the teacher is, he/she will have undertaken a great deal of work beforehand in order to ensure that the class is run smoothly.

CHAPTER 8

Challenging behaviour

INTRODUCTION

According to Emerson (1995) there are over one million people in Europe, North America and Australasia who have learning disabilities and additional challenging behaviours. As Zarkowska and Clements (1994) observe, many of these behaviours are similar to those found in the general population (e.g. temper tantrums and aggression). However, others tend to be associated with people with learning disabilities, for example rocking, masturbating, stripping in public, face slapping or hand biting. These behaviours can be extremely distressing for staff, parents and the people themselves. Having a child with challenging behaviour is one of the main causes for the break-up of families and/or for the pupil being removed to residential provision. Prevention, early detection and intervention are crucial factors in helping to minimize the long-term incidence and effects on the people themselves, their families and carers. Schools, therefore, have a vital part to play in this process for, if challenging behaviour in pupils is reduced, this will have long-term benefits as they move into adulthood.

Approaches to working with pupils who have challenging behaviour are derived from the same behavioural principles which underpin the teaching techniques that are aimed at helping pupils to develop new skills and knowledge. These were discussed in Chapters 3, 4 and 5. In particular, to be successful in helping a pupil with behaviour problems it is almost always necessary to observe carefully the antecedents and setting conditions, to set clear targets, to use reinforcement in a sensitive and carefully planned way and to record accurately. There is therefore a considerable overlap between the teaching techniques that have been discussed in the chapters mentioned above and the approaches referred to in this chapter. However, these approaches should also be applied carefully, bearing in mind some of the principles of Gentle Teaching (McGee, 1992), in particular the need for 'unconditional valuing and the focus on mutual change'.

In view of the extremely distressing nature of some problem behaviour, parents and school staff often need a great deal of support and guidance when working with pupils with challenging behaviour. There have been occasions when totally inappropriate handling techniques have been adopted, some of which border on cruelty. These almost always occur when a parent or staff member feels unsupported and out of control of the situation and may be an instant reaction to a particular event. Senior staff therefore have a responsibility to establish systems for supporting their colleagues at all times.

In this chapter we discuss the definition, incidence and causes of challenging behaviour in pupils with learning difficulties. This is followed by a review of some general guidelines for prevention and intervention at the whole school and individual level and a discussion of some specific management strategies.

DEFINING CHALLENGING BEHAVIOUR

Emerson (1995) defines challenging behaviour as:

> culturally abnormal behaviour(s) of such intensity, frequency or duration that the physical safety of the person or others is likely to be placed in serious jeopardy, or behaviour which is likely to seriously limit use of, or result in the person being denied access to, ordinary community facilities. (p. 4)

For some years the phrase 'challenging behaviour' has been adopted, as the term implies that the behaviours are challenging for all those who live and work with the pupil and that they also provide a challenge for those whose duty it is to provide adequate services. Thus the problems are not necessarily seen as implying psychological or psychiatric disturbance. Indeed some challenging behaviours in children can be an understandable reaction to events occurring in their life, for example extreme moodiness following the death of a parent. Therefore, when planning for intervention, it is important to consider the contribution that the pupil's environment, and the attitudes and behaviour of the people who live and work with the pupil, may have in causing the behaviour.

There are a number of behaviours coming within the above definition which are likely to be referred to as challenging. These can be roughly divided into the following: nuisance behaviours, anti-social (aggressive) behaviours, self-injurious behaviours, stereotype behaviours. Examples of behaviours which fall into these areas are provided below. However, they are only intended as a rough guide and frequently behaviours may fall into more than one area.

Nuisance behaviours. These behaviours are unlikely to pose a physical threat to the pupil, his/her environment or the people in it. They are more likely to cause embarrassment and distress or they may be extremely irritating and threaten the smooth running of an organization. Examples of such behaviours are as follows: screaming, stripping, swearing, making repetitive noises, masturbation, running away, temper tantrums, non-compliance, extreme overactivity, phobias, stealing.

Aggressive behaviours. These behaviours are directed at other people and/or property and, as the term implies, they can cause serious damage. They include: hitting, hair pulling, throwing, kicking, biting, fighting, scratching.

Self-injurious behaviours. These behaviours can be extremely distressing for parents and teachers as they often appear at first sight to be entirely functionless, painful and literally self-destructive. Such behaviours could include: head banging, face slapping, hand biting, eye gouging, skin scratching, eating inedible objects.

Stereotyped behaviours. These behaviours are frequently repetitive and may also appear to serve no function. They include: rocking, hand flapping, regurgitation.

Many of the behaviours listed above are not associated specifically with pupils who have learning difficulties, for example running away and non-compliance. However, other behaviours, for example self-injurious and stereotyped behaviours and some specific nuisance behaviours (stripping and uncontrolled masturbation) tend to be associated with this group, particularly pupils with severe and profound learning difficulties.

Some of these more severe behaviours may be completely unfamiliar to inexperienced staff and, unless they are prepared and given adequate support, the behaviours can cause considerable distress. This happened on one occasion, known to the author, when a newly appointed female nursery nurse discovered that a male teenage student with profound and multiple learning difficulties had masturbated to climax in a corner of the classroom and that she was expected to 'clean him up'. Schools need to ensure that appropriate systems are put in place to support staff who have to manage in such situations.

Lowe and Felce (1995) point out that the majority of attention is given to challenging behaviours which cause disruption to the environment and the people in it. However, some behaviours, for example stereotyped behaviours (e.g. rocking) and extreme social withdrawal, may receive less adult attention as they cause less disruption; these behaviours can have a 'pervasive, detrimental effect on quality of life and development' and are therefore just as challenging.

The social construction of challenging behaviour

It goes without saying that teachers, parents and other carers are almost always placed in positions of power over all pupils, including pupils with learning difficulties. This means that they are responsible, whether they like it or not, for setting the 'rules' or standards of behaviour that they deem to be acceptable from the pupils they are looking after. They therefore define what is and is not challenging behaviour. These definitions may depend on the composition and function of a particular setting and on the beliefs and attitudes of those who are in charge. One would expect the rules and expected standards of behaviour to be different between a family home and a school. In addition there may be differences between mainstream and special schools in the standards of behaviour they expect. There may also be differences of opinion between the staff of a school as to what behaviour is acceptable and what is 'challenging' – for example in the level of noise they will tolerate in a classroom.

There is also a tendency for non-disabled people to tolerate unusual behaviours in pupils with disabilities and explain the behaviour in terms of the disability – 'He can't help behaving in that way, it's because he has X-syndrome.' Attitudes such as these can result in such behaviours being ignored or even reinforced with no attempt being made to change them. It has been argued that special schools fall into this trap and expect poorer standards of behaviour than would be tolerated in a mainstream school and that, as a result, the behaviours deteriorate and it becomes even harder to integrate pupils with disabilities into mainstream schools.

It can be seen from the above discussion that there is no objective definition of challenging behaviour. Such behaviour has to be viewed within the context of the settings where it takes place and the values, attitudes and beliefs of the people working within those settings. Behaviours are described as problematic if they cause problems for those who live and work with the individual with the 'problem'. They may not be a problem for the pupils themselves.

PREVALENCE OF CHALLENGING BEHAVIOUR

In a summary of studies investigating the prevalence of pupils with SLD who also have challenging behaviour Harris (1995) suggests that the figure lies between 10 per cent and 15 per cent. However he acknowledges that it is extremely difficult to get accurate figures mainly because studies use different definitions of challenging behaviour. In a survey of SLD schools in Hampshire Norgate (1994) found that seventy-nine pupils were identified as 'exhibiting a broad range of difficult behaviour' of whom seventeen were felt to display 'severe challenging behaviour'. In Kiernan and Kiernan's (1994) survey of SLD schools 22 per cent of pupils were identified as presenting some degree of challenge including 8 per cent who were identified as presenting a significant challenge.

When comparing the prevalence of the types of challenging behaviour that the schools reported it is noticeable that, apart from aggression, which was top in the studies by Harris and Kiernan and Kiernan, and second in Norgate's survey, there appears to be little agreement between them as to the prevalence of the types of behaviour that teachers find challenging. In the Kiernans' study, social disruption, temper tantrums, self-injurious behaviour and physical disruption featured almost as highly as aggression. Harris however found that aggression was by far the most prominent with self-injury, shouting etc., distractibility and damaging property coming a long way behind and temper tantrums hardly featuring at all. In Norgate's research teachers put 'demanding' behaviour at the top of their list with stereotypical behaviour also featuring highly and self-injury hardly featuring at all.

Other factors of note are that boys are more likely to be identified than girls (Norgate, *op. cit.*), particularly for more severe challenging behaviour (Kiernan and Kiernan, *op. cit.*). Such behaviours increase with age and peak during the age range 15 to 34 (Oliver *et al*, 1987). Generally, the more severe the intellectual impairment the greater the chance that a pupil's behaviour will be challenging.

According to Emerson (1995) relatively little is known about the progress made by pupils with challenging behaviour. However, such evidence that exists is not encouraging. Murphy *et al* (1993), for example, in a follow-up study of fifty-four individuals whose severe self-injurious behaviour had resulted in them needing to wear a protective device, found that the mean age of onset was seven years of age and the mean duration of the behaviour was fourteen years. Stenfert-Kroese and Fleming (1993) reported that only one of a group of seventeen pupils with challenging behaviour showed no challenging behaviour in each of the following three years. Robertson *et al* (1996) interviewed the parents of forty-four pupils who had previously attended Beech Tree residential school for pupils with severely challenging behaviours. Although parents indicated significant reductions in challenging behaviour while the pupil was placed at the school and the majority reported that these positive changes continued once the pupil had left, as many as 21 per cent stated that there was a deterioration in challenging behaviour following placement at the school. Emerson (1995) suggests that the available evidence about the long-term outcomes for people with challenging behaviour, in particular self-injurious behaviour, indicates that, even with the help of highly staffed specialist services, such behaviours are extremely resistant to change.

CAUSES OF CHALLENGING BEHAVIOUR

Zarkowska and Clements (1994) point out that it is unusual to find a simple cause of challenging behaviour in people with severe learning difficulties and that there are a number of overlapping factors to consider.

It is known, for example, that some specific syndromes are associated with an increased likelihood of challenging behaviour. For example people with Lesch-Nyhan Syndrome are prone to self-injurious behaviour, specifically hand and lip biting (Nyhan, 1994). Harris (1992) reports a high incidence of hand-wringing in people with Rett's Syndrome. A greater than expected prevalence of attention deficits and stereotyping is found in pupils with Fragile X Syndrome (Lachiewicz *et al*, 1994). Just what the factors are within the condition or syndrome which specifically cause the challenging behaviour remains uncertain and, for an individual pupil with one of the above syndromes, it may be just as possible that the cause of the behaviour problems relates to the way he/she has been managed.

There are in fact many syndromes associated with severe learning difficulty which are not linked to any specific type of challenging behaviour or with its prevalence. It is far more likely, therefore, that a pupil's challenging behaviour will have developed as a result of the way he/she has been handled and not be associated with the specific syndrome from which he/she suffers. Zarkowska and Clements (*op. cit.*) refer to environmental factors such as the quality of care, the level of tension and interpersonal conflict within a setting and inconsistency in handling as being key factors in causing problem behaviours to arise. It is also the case that pupils placed in unstimulating environments in which they have little to do are more likely to develop stereotyped behaviours. Indeed the phrase 'the Devil makes work for idle hands', often used in reference to discussing problem behaviour in all pupils, equally refers to pupils with learning difficulties.

One further issue to consider when discussing the causes of challenging behaviour is the need to distinguish between the form and the function of the behaviour. Describing the form of the behaviour (e.g. the intensity, frequency) may provide little information about its function for the pupil, i.e. what is he/she trying to achieve by the challenging behaviour? For example, is the pupil frustrated at being unable to communicate, is he/she trying to gain someone's attention? Understanding the function of the behaviour is crucial to learning about the cause and may lead to appropriate intervention strategies being developed (see Remington, 1991). We will return to this point later in the chapter when discussing the importance of observation when planning intervention.

Finally, for some self-injurious and stereotyped behaviours (e.g. rocking), the factors which caused the behaviour to begin in the first place may be different from those which cause it to be maintained. For example, a pupil who is left with nothing to do may revert to rocking or nail biting, perhaps to provide some stimulation. The behaviour is initially caused by inappropriate management within the pupil's setting. However, if the behaviour is allowed to persist, it is possible that it will lead to the release of B-endorphin which, according to Emerson (1995) has 'analgesic, antinocicoptive and euphoria-inducing properties' and therefore acts as a powerful reinforcer for the pupil. Once such reinforcers begin to operate, it becomes increasingly difficult to plan successful interventions as these reinforcers may override all other competing ones which are then introduced.

Up to now this chapter has discussed definitions, prevalence, types and causes of challenging behaviours in pupils with learning difficulties. For the remainder we shall consider some key factors which underpin methods of prevention and intervention in this complex area. There is insufficient space to provide detailed practical suggestions on specific techniques, and readers are referred to McBrien and Felce (1994) and Zarkowska and Clements (1994) for more complete guidance. The sections that follow cover the following areas:

- general guidelines for senior staff in schools and residential establishments;
- general guidelines for teachers;
- some specific intervention strategies;
- the Department of Health's guidelines on *Permissible Forms of Control* (DOH, 1993) and its impact on professional practice;
- a brief review of the use of medication to help pupils with challenging behaviour.

GUIDELINES FOR HEADTEACHERS AND SENIOR MANAGERS

The idea of developing guidelines on how to help pupils who have challenging behaviour is not new. Indeed the DFE *Circular on Pupil Behaviour and Discipline* (DFE, 1994c) reminds all schools of the need to develop whole school behaviour policies, and offers guidance on how these should be developed and on their possible contents. Many special schools for pupils with learning difficulties and emotional and behavioural problems have also developed consistent handling strategies for managing individual pupils which are informed by their discipline policy. Finally all local authorities produce guidelines on child protection procedures.

Much of the contents of this and the following section may appear at first sight to be common sense and to be stating the obvious. But common sense is not always easy to apply! We can all think of times when we have behaved inappropriately and have made matters worse either professionally as teachers or in our personal life. How many of us can honestly say that we have treated pupils fairly at all times or that we have always behaved calmly and rationally? With hindsight 'common sense' would tell us that we had acted stupidly and we may privately or even publicly express regret. However, even with the benefit of hindsight and prolonged reflection, we may still behave the same way again on another occasion. We, like our pupils, are only human and can act inappropriately without thinking things through. Therefore, although these guidelines may appear to be common sense, they are an attempt to help practitioners to behave in a fair, rational and planned way when helping pupils with challenging behaviour and so reduce the chance that we may act hastily and without thinking.

Underpinning the following guidelines is the need for schools to create a positive ethos. The DFE *Draft Circular on Pupil Behaviour and Discipline* emphasises the role of the governing body in this respect. Ethos is a word which is often used but hard to define. Rutter *et al* (1979), referring to mainstream secondary education, used the term to describe schools which had developed policies and created an atmosphere in which pupils and parents feel welcome and where rewards rather than punishments are used to encourage learning and good behaviour. The following guidelines should help schools to develop a positive ethos although the uniqueness of each setting means that the factors in one school which contribute towards a positive ethos may be different from another.

1. Develop, monitor and review whole school policies for helping pupils with challenging behaviour.
The DFE *Draft Circular on Pupils' Behaviour and Discipline* urges schools to produce whole school behaviour policies and provides guidance on how these should be developed. It suggests that the policy should contain the following features:

- it should be based on a clear and defensible set of principles and values;
- mutual respect is a useful starting point;
- the policy should encourage good behaviour rather than simply punish bad behaviour;
- the policy should be specific to the school;
- rules should be kept to a minimum;
- the reasons for each rule should be obvious; and
- wherever possible rules should be expressed in positive constructive terms (DFE, 1994c, pp. 12–13).

It also suggests the stages which schools might go through when developing their policy. These stress the need for all staff to be involved and for parents and pupils to be consulted. This 'bottom up' approach, if successfully applied, will take time but should result in the policy being successfully implemented. However it is important for it to be regularly monitored and reviewed.

2. Create an atmosphere which encourages openness in discussions between class teachers and senior managers
It is in the nature of the job that headteachers and senior managers are experienced teachers, better paid than class teachers and in a position of power over their junior colleagues. It is not uncommon for hard-pressed class teachers to feel resentful about what they may perceive to be the 'protected' and 'less pressurized' role of the senior manager. Remarks such as 'It's all very well for them to tell me what to do but how often do they have to teach a pupil who continually makes loud and uncontrollable noises' are not unknown. Managers more often than not deal with the consequences of misbehaviour (for example arrange and chair a case conference) and not with the behaviour itself. Therefore, underpinning these guidelines is the need for senior managers to be sensitive to criticisms of this sort and to do everything possible to counteract them.

If a member of staff is experiencing problems managing a class or an individual pupil, he/she should feel able to discuss the situation openly with a senior member of staff. Too often class teachers have soldiered on alone for fear of being made to feel a failure if they discuss their problems with others. It is not necessarily a sign of weakness if a teacher experiences discipline problems and indeed *all* teachers, even those who are promoted to senior positions, will have experienced difficulties at the start of their career. It is therefore vital for senior managers to support their staff who are having problems. They need to make themselves available to offer help and to be proactive in supporting staff who have hitherto not asked for it. This requires senior staff to possess a high degree of sensitivity and good interpersonal skills.

3. Have clearly defined roles for staff.
Staff should know who has responsibility for all aspects of helping pupils with challenging behaviour. This could include responsibility for dealing with outside agencies, for contacting parents, for dealing with crises.

4. Establish teams of staff who work well together.
Thomas (1992) has stressed the value and importance of effective classroom teamwork. In the vast majority of schools and classes for pupils with learning difficulties there will be at least two members of staff. Effective teamwork can dramatically reduce the incidence of classroom disruption. It is therefore vital for senior staff to as far as possible establish teams which work well together.

5. Establish a mechanism whereby regular meetings can be held to plan and review programmes for individuals who are causing concern.
Whenever a school is concerned about a pupil's behaviour it is important to develop a consistent handling strategy to plan a programme of intervention. Such a policy should be planned at a meeting of relevant staff and outside agencies, the parents and if possible the pupil. Regular meetings should then be held to monitor and review the programme. Many special schools have already developed systems for implementing consistent handling strategies.

6. Develop good working relationships with other agencies.
All schools for pupils with learning difficulties have access to a wide range of different agencies, many of whom work regularly in the school. It is vitally important for senior staff to get to know the agencies which are available, to have regular meetings with key staff from them and to develop a working relationship which is based on trust and a sharing of knowledge and expertise.

7. *Ensure that there are sufficient opportunities for staff development and training.*

McEvoy *et al* (1991) and Pyke (1990) stress the importance of ongoing staff training in this area. Senior staff in schools should support in-service training by making sure that their in-service budget is sufficient to cover the need, by drawing on the expertise of support services in the area and by liaising with their local Institute of Higher Education.

GUIDELINES FOR TEACHERS AND OTHER 'FRONT-LINE' STAFF

On first reading, the following guidelines may appear somewhat mechanical and dispassionate. Inevitably they do not reflect the heat, feelings and emotion that can be felt by both staff and pupils when dealing with a pupil who is displaying severe behaviour problems. Events can move extremely quickly in a crisis and it is a lot to ask of staff to behave in a way which is consistent with the guidelines. Therefore these guidelines are not, and could never be, the whole answer. Although they should inform good practice for the majority of the time, there will always be occasions when the procedures to follow when an incident occurs may not be adhered to. Hopefully the consequences of ignoring or forgetting guidelines will not always be catastrophic but this depends on the nature of the guidelines which have not been followed.

1. Involve everybody in planning intervention programmes.

'Everybody' means the teachers who know the pupil best, other relevant professionals, the parents and, if possible, the pupil. The aim should be to arrive at a position where everybody agrees about the nature of the problem, the causes, and what to do about it. This may not be easy to achieve but, as a starting point, it is important for everyone to get together to discuss the problem so that the risk of someone feeling excluded is reduced and there is a greater chance that everybody will co-operate with the programme. These meetings need to be handled carefully as feelings may be running high, particularly if the people involved have different views about the extent and/or cause of the problem. Issues such as where such meetings should be held and who chairs them are also important. They should not be seen as an opportunity for one party to blame the other. Parents, in particular, should not be made to feel overawed by the occasion and should take part in the discussion as equal partners.

2. *At all times pupils should be engaged in useful activities which are of interest to them and at their ability level.*

To implement this guideline staff should develop individual programme plans for all pupils which:

- are based on an accurate assessment of each pupil's attainment on all areas of the curriculum;
- is broad, balanced and relevant;
- takes account of the wishes of the pupils and the parents;
- combines high quality individual and group teaching;
- takes account of the resources available in the class and school.

In summary, therefore, if staff successfully employ the teaching techniques referred to in Chapters 4 and 5, if the curriculum is appropriate (Chapter 6) and if the classroom is managed successfully (Chapter 7), the chances that pupils will display challenging behaviour are dramatically reduced. As implied earlier in this chapter, if pupils are busy doing useful things then they are less likely to misbehave. The guideline is a key preventative strategy and demonstrates that the successful education of pupils with learning difficulties depends on an integrated approach being adopted which takes account of all aspects of their learning and development.

Harris (1995) also stresses the importance of this guideline when he states that staff should 'introduce planned activities matched to pupils' strengths and weaknesses'.

3. *Describe behaviour precisely.*

It is important to describe the behaviour(s) which are causing concern as precisely as possible. Statements such as 'He's always noisy' or 'She's very unhappy' tell us little about the behaviour and hence provide few clues as to how one might help. Similarly it is also important to be precise as to the level of behaviour we are hoping to achieve. This is exactly the same as writing target behaviours referred to in Chapter 4. If staff, parents and pupils are clear about them, it is easier to achieve the required goal.

4. *Observe behaviour carefully.*

Having described the behaviour accurately, the next step is to observe the antecedents, setting conditions and consequences. This will help to gain an understanding of the exact nature of the behaviour, when it occurs, with whom, and to what extent. It will also provide clues as to what triggers and maintains the behaviour. In this way it is possible to understand the function of the behaviour for the pupil. For example is he/she frustrated at not being able to communicate; is he/she behaving inappropriately to gain other people's attention; does the behaviour communicate fear or apprehension? Gaining a more complete understanding of the function of the behaviour may give significant clues as to what might be done to improve the situation.

5. Be explicit and realistic about when the desired behaviour could be achieved.
Don't be too ambitious; make sure everybody, especially the pupil, knows precisely what the programme is hoping to achieve and has agreed to implement it. When trying to change behaviour it is better to set modest targets which could be achieved in a relatively short space of time, e.g. two weeks. In this way there is a greater chance of achieving success and this may increase the chances that other behaviours can be changed as well.

6. Rewards work better than punishment.
This is a key finding from all research on helping pupils with challenging behaviour (see for example McBrien and Felce, 1994; Presland, 1991; Harris 1995). Rewards help to promote a positive ethos in the school and are likely to contribute to building good relationships between a teacher and his/her pupils. As we have seen earlier in this book, rewards are an effective way of encouraging learning and in the same way they can be used to develop appropriate forms of behaviour. It is therefore important to establish the rewards which the pupil likes and to use them contingently as he/she develops the desired behaviour. The use of rewards will be referred to again when we discuss specific intervention techniques.

Punishment involves the loss of something a pupil likes or the presentation of something which he/she finds aversive. All parents and teachers throughout the world employ punishment and there are occasions when its use is unavoidable. Some of the techniques referred to later in this chapter could be described as punishment and will only be effective if they are combined with rewards. Using punishment alone may create a negative atmosphere between the teacher and pupil which is not conducive to effective learning.

7. Be calm.
This guideline is not always easy to implement, particularly for pupils whose behaviour is quite extreme. However its importance cannot be over-stressed. Teachers who are calm are more likely to be in control of themselves and the situation. Losing control may result in teachers saying or doing things they may regret.

8. *Make intervention strategies explicit.*

These should be clear to everybody and include information on who should do what when undesirable behaviour occurs, what rewards will be used, how the programme will be monitored, when it will be reviewed and by whom and what support is required. The strategy should be *applied consistently;* in general desirable behaviour should be rewarded and inappropriate behaviour dealt with in an ethically acceptable manner which does not affect relationships with the pupil(s).

SOME SPECIFIC TECHNIQUES FOR HELPING PUPILS WITH CHALLENGING BEHAVIOUR

The following is a brief overview of some specific techniques which can be used when helping pupils with challenging behaviour. None of them should be used in isolation but should be part of an overall programme which has been discussed with other staff, the parents and if possible the pupil. Strategies 4, 5 and 6 could be described as a form of punishment and are therefore controversial and need to be used with extreme care.

1. *Change the setting.*

This is a preventative and non-intrusive strategy which would normally derive from careful observation of the antecedents and, in particular, the setting conditions. If these observations indicate clearly and consistently when the behaviour is most and least likely to occur, it may be possible to simply change the setting and, as a result, the problem behaviour will not occur. For example it may be possible to move the pupil to another class or to alter the seating arrangements in the existing class. In one example, known to the author, a pupil who almost always arrived at school in a distressed and unmanageable state, was taken to the medical room for the first half hour of the day. After this period she was able to enter the classroom in a much calmer frame of mind.

2. *Ignore the unacceptable behaviour.*

If the observation indicates that a pupil behaves in an inappropriate way in order to gain attention and if the behaviour does not disrupt others and is not dangerous, it may be possible to eliminate it by simply ignoring it. This is sometimes referred to as 'Planned ignoring'. Examples of behaviour which might be ignored include making silly noises, running out of class, and swearing. It is important to remember that, at the beginning of a programme of planned ignoring, the pupil will expect a reaction from the adult and may therefore continue with the behaviour at an increased level in the expectation that he/she will eventually get a response. At this time it is very important to keep ignoring the pupil so that eventually he/she realizes that the behaviour will not bring a response.

3. *Reward appropriate behaviour.*

This strategy has already been alluded to in the above guidelines. It is clearly a crucial strategy and should be used in *combination with all other strategies*. In general it is important to reward all behaviour which is desirable and incompatible with the inappropriate behaviour. For example a pupil who frequently runs out of class could be rewarded for sitting still; a pupil who bites his/her hand could be rewarded for drawing or playing with puzzles. As in all strategies the effect of the rewards used should be carefully monitored. We have seen earlier in this book (Chapter 5) that it is not always easy to determine what rewards work for pupils with learning difficulties and that some pupils frequently change their preferences for rewards.

4. *Time-out.*

A great deal has been written about the use and misuse of Time-out procedures (see for example Mace *et al*, 1986; Murphy and Oliver, 1987). Essentially the term means 'Time-out from reinforcement' and as such is supposed to indicate that, when the procedure is in operation, the pupil receives no rewards. In effect it is a form of punishment and therefore needs to be used with extreme care.

There are two forms of Time-out. In the first, the rewards are removed from the pupil and, in the second, the pupil is removed from the reinforcing situation.

The first form of Time-out can be used in an individual teaching session when a pupil displays irritating behaviours such as fiddling with the teaching materials or repetitive tapping of the table. The teacher should give a firm signal (e.g. 'Stop tapping!') and if the pupil does not respond, the materials are removed from the table and the teacher turns his/her back on the pupil. When the pupil settles down the teacher resumes teaching. This form of Time-out can be quite effective for mildly irritating behaviours similar to the examples given above. However some pupils' behaviour can deteriorate during the Time-out period – they may leave their chair or poke the teacher in the back. If this occurs, alternative strategies may be needed.

In the second form of Time-out the pupil's behaviour is such that he/she needs to be removed to another place. This frequently happens in mainstream classes when a pupil is told to stand or sit in a corner or leave the classroom. In schools for pupils with learning difficulties this form of Time-out is usually taken to mean that the pupil is removed to another room where he/she is left to cool off and calm down. If it is used properly it will be part of an overall behavioural management plan which has been fully discussed with staff, parents and the pupil. When the pupil displays the specified behaviour which will be 'Timed out', he/she will be given a verbal signal (e.g. 'Stop screaming!') and, if the behaviour continues, he/she will be taken to a small, well-lit and ventilated room containing little or no furniture and told to stay there until he/she has calmed down. A few seconds after this has happened the pupil will be told that he/she can return to the classroom when he/she feels ready to do so. In the past the pupil could have been locked in the room, with a member of staff remaining outside until he/she has calmed down.

This form of Time-out is controversial for a number of reasons. First, the pupil may not wish to go to the Time-out room and will need to be placed there forcibly. This may require more than one staff member, it may take some time and be distressing and possibly dangerous for all concerned, including the pupil. Some pupils may be too strong to move. Second, pupils may deliberately behave badly in order to get placed in the Time-out room as, while there, they do not have to engage in a classroom activity that they dislike. Third, there have been occasions when the technique has been applied incorrectly, with pupils being left for many hours in a locked room with no staff being available to check on their behaviour. Indeed, the Department of Health's guidelines (DOH 1993), discussed below, make it clear that it is illegal to lock a pupil in a room. Time-out is also inappropriate for self-injurious behaviour as, unless such behaviour is attention-seeking, there is no reason why the pupil should not continue with the behaviour while in the Time-out room.

Despite some problems with this more extreme form of Time-out, it can be an effective technique as it provides the rest of the group with a break and the teachers with strategy for controlling the behaviour and removing it from view. Furthermore, many pupils appreciate the opportunity to calm down in a quiet room away from other people.

5. Restraint.

There are two main forms of restraint. The first is a commonsense technique in which a pupil is forcibly restrained by one or more members of staff to prevent a pupil from attacking other staff, pupils or property. To refrain from using restraint could result in serious damage being done. Although there are many occasions when staff have no alternative than to restrain a pupil, the technique is still controversial and open to some of the problems referred to above in relation to Time-out. In particular the pupil may be quite strong and there may not be sufficient staff available to restrain him/her. There is always a risk that staff or the pupil may be hurt. Alternatively, the act of restraining can be quite reinforcing for some pupils. Teachers also need to stay calm and in control and this is not always easy when struggling to restrain a pupil who is screaming, has dragged you onto the floor and is trying to bite you!

The second form of restraint can be used to stop or prevent self-injurious behaviour. For example, if a pupil frequently bites his/her hand, the arms can be placed in splints. Although this will prevent hand biting, it may cause the pupil some discomfort and will almost certainly prevent him/her from engaging in many other activities. The use of such restraints should be avoided if at all possible but there may be occasions when one is left with no choice but to use them for some of the time.

The use of restraint is discussed in more detail below when we review the Department of Health's Guidelines. In addition, Harris (1996) has provided a comprehensive review of the literature on the use of restraint procedures with children and adults. Although there are occasions when these procedures, if carefully and systematically applied, can be effective, Harris considers that 'any form of restraint should be viewed as a risky strategy which may have unpredictable consequences for participants'. He also concludes that there is very little evidence of the extent to which restraint is used by staff working with children and adults with learning difficulties.

6. Overcorrection.

Overcorrection (Foxx and Azrin, 1973) is a technique in which the pupil is required to behave in an exaggerated or 'overcorrect' way which is incompatible with the inappropriate behaviour.

There are two kinds of overcorrection, restitutional and positive practice. Restitutional overcorrection is typically used for pupils who may throw materials and furniture around the classroom. As in Time-out the pupil is given a signal (e.g. 'Pick them up') and if there is no response, he/she is made to pick them up with the teacher physically guiding the hand to all the objects that have been thrown. To make the situation 'overcorrect' the pupil is also made to tidy up other parts of the classroom as well, even though he/she did not make them untidy in the first place.

Positive practice overcorrection tends to be used for self-injurious behaviours such as head banging or hand biting. Once again the pupil is given a signal (e.g. 'Stop biting') and, if he/she does not respond, another instruction is given (e.g. 'Put your arms by your side') and this is followed by the teacher physically guiding the pupil's hands until they are by his/her side. They are then held there until the pupil relaxes.

Both restitutional and positive practice overcorrection are contro-versial as the use of physical guidance can quickly become a form of restraint with all the associated problems which have already been mentioned. It also takes a long time to implement and may disrupt the other pupils. Given these difficulties it is a technique that is only used rarely in schools for pupils with learning difficulties.

THE DEPARTMENT OF HEALTH'S GUIDANCE, DOH (1993)

As the foregoing discussion has implied, no matter how good a school's preventative strategies are, how well a setting is managed, how well resourced and how high the morale of the staff, we still may need to use strategies which involve restricting pupils' liberty, hold-ing or restraining them. These strategies are potentially open to abuse. In order to advise staff on these matters the Department of Health has issued a circular entitled *Guidance on Permissible Forms of Control in Pupils' Residential Care* (DOH, 1993). The guidance is derived from and builds on Volume 4 of the Children Act, Guidance and Regulations. The DfEE has sent it to all independent schools catering for pupils with special needs, to all non-maintained special schools and 'endorses the advice and guidance offered'. Lyon (1994a/b) has reviewed the impact of these guidelines and focuses on the occasions when, under the Children Act, it may be justifiable to use restraint procedures with children who have learning difficulties and challenging behaviour.

The DOH guidelines focus on strategies to help pupils whose behaviour is extremely violent and aggressive where people or prop-erty may be damaged. Although they do not state this, the impression is that the DOH believes these kinds of behaviours would not nor-mally be found in mainstream schools.

The decision to make provisions in the Children Act and produce guidelines on permissible forms of control arose from adverse publicity on the management of pupils with behaviour problems, notably that which led to the 'Pin Down' enquiry into methods that were used to control children's behaviour in residential settings in Staffordshire. Hence it is important to remember that, although these guidelines apply to all professionals who work with children in any setting, they arose out of unacceptable practices employed by residential workers in children's homes.

The main focus of the guidelines is on acceptable and effective techniques to deal with violent and aggressive behaviour. The key point is that techniques such as *physical restraint* or those which are designed to *restrict liberty* can only be used *if there is a risk that the child will damage himself/herself, other people or property.* In no other circumstances should children's liberty be restricted or physical restraint used.

The guidelines then proceed to discuss alternative methods, in particular using 'physical presence' and 'holding' before going on to describe how physical restraint should be applied when the pupil is in danger of injuring him/herself or property and the implications of the regulations on the restriction of liberty.

1. Use of physical presence.
This can be used to reinforce the staff's authority and concern. Staff may stand in the way of a pupil who is trying to run out of class or place a hand on his/her arm. It should be used 'in the context of trying to engage the pupil in discussion about the significance and implications of his behaviour' (page 16). If the pupil physically resists, another technique will be needed.

2. Holding.
The DOH guidelines attempt to distinguish between 'holding' and 'physical restraint'. In general, holding is permissible as it involves less force and therefore can be used even if there is no risk of the pupil damaging him/herself, others or property. The distinction between the two techniques is not easy to define. The guidelines state that the main factor separating one from the other is 'the manner of intervention and the *degree of force applied.* Physical restraint uses the degree of force necessary to *prevent* a pupil harming himself or others or property. Holding would *discourage* but in itself would not prevent such an action', (pages 16–17; emphases are taken from the guidelines).

The guidelines suggest that holding may be an appropriate technique to use when guiding a child away from a confrontation with another pupil or when insisting on holding a pupil's hand to cross a road.

When applying the holding technique the member of staff should:

1. know the pupil and explain why holding is being used;
2. use another method if the pupil forcibly resists, in consultation with other staff;
3. ensure that sexual expectations or feelings are not being aroused.

3. Physical restraint.
As already stated, physical restraint can only be used if the pupil's behaviour is likely to damage him/herself or property. This technique may be used to prevent a pupil from attacking someone or from

smashing furniture or if he/she is threatening to run out of the building with the suspected intention of damaging others or property.

When using physical restraint staff should:

1. give a warning that physical restraint will be used;
2. use the 'minimum' force necessary;
3. ensure other staff are present;
4. gradually withdraw the restraint to allow the pupil to regain self-control;
5. record the action taken;
6. discuss the incident with the line manager;
7. discuss the incident with the pupil involved.

The above suggestions, though helpful, may in practice be extremely difficult to apply. It is likely that a technique such as physical restraint will be needed when the situation is tense and charged with emotion. In this atmosphere staff have to make snap judgements and it may not be possible or even desirable to wait until another member of staff is present, as by the time this happens, someone might have been hurt or property damaged.

4. Restriction of liberty.
Under section 25 of the Children Act children's liberty can only be restricted by placing them in a community home with secure accommodation approved by the Secretary of State. Such children are likely to have committed criminal offences and/or to have a record of persistent absconding and whilst absconding are likely to suffer 'significant harm'. In no other circumstances is it permissible to forcibly restrict a child's liberty.

For all but the tiny minority of children who are placed in secure units it is therefore illegal to lock a pupil in a room even for a very short period of time. This practice, which is sometimes part of a Time-out procedure, has been relatively common in day and residential schools for pupils with severe learning difficulties and challenging behaviour and is now clearly illegal. The DOH guidelines are ambiguous about measures to restrict pupils' liberty which fall short of locking a pupil in a room, e.g. whether it is acceptable to shut a pupil in a room with a member of staff standing on the other side of the door to prevent an escape. The legality of such measures will 'ultimately be determined by the courts'. It suggests that such action may on occasions be necessary to prevent injury or damage to people or property and urges local authorities to seek legal advice when formulating their guidance to staff.

Physical restraint, using the guidelines summarized above, should only be used to restrict a pupil's liberty if failure to do so may result in injury to people or property. If there is no reason to believe that this will occur, then other methods short of using physical restraint must be used.

The law on the restriction of liberty enshrined in the Children Act has caused some problems for staff who are involved in teaching and caring for pupils with severe challenging behaviour (Jones, personal communication; Wolkind, 1993). Techniques such as Time-out have proved to be effective when used carefully with the agreement of all parties. Many residential establishments have had to rethink their strategies and guidelines to take account of the provisions of the Act.

THE USE OF MEDICATION IN THE MANAGEMENT OF PUPILS WITH CHALLENGING BEHAVIOUR

One commonly used strategy that doctors, paediatricians and psychiatrists may use to control behaviour is medication. At the present time there appears to be little evidence as to the extent of its use with pupils with learning difficulties whose behaviour is challenging. However, in the adult population there is evidence that up to 50 per cent of people with challenging behaviour receive some form of medication (see Parry, 1993; Kiernan and Qureshi, 1993). Emerson (1995) expresses concern about the use of medication, suggesting that it is not particularly effective, that there are often unpleasant side-effects, that frequently inappropriate doses have been prescribed and that reducing or eliminating medication does not always result in increasing levels of challenging behaviour. In schools it is essential for teachers to know whether a pupil is on medication, the aims of the intervention, when it will be reviewed, the likely side-effects, what the dose should be, who should administer it and when this should take place. There have been occasions when a fractious parent who has become completely exhausted by the behaviour of his/her child, has administered an extra large dose in order to tranquillize the child. If schools are fully aware of the procedure for administering the medications, the risk of this occurring is reduced.

CONCLUSION

This chapter has reviewed some of the key issues concerned with the management of pupils with challenging behaviour. The topic is complex and a great deal has been written about it in the literature. It is important to remember that pupils' behaviour can be extremely distressing for parents, teachers and other professionals. Intervention should be conducted in an atmosphere where everyone feels supported and where the rights and wishes of all concerned, including the pupil, are uppermost in people's minds. When planning intervention it is important for everybody to be calm and systematic, for individual programme plans to be relevant to the pupil's needs, for interventions to be based, wherever possible, on rewarding appropriate behaviour and for all those involved to work well together.

CHAPTER 9

Integration: conceptual issues and current provision

INTRODUCTION

As the integration of pupils with learning difficulties is an extremely complex and important topic, two chapters have been devoted to discussing the issues. Further reviews of current developments in the integration debate can be found by consulting Sebba and Ainscow (1996a) and Farrell (1996). The aim of both these chapters, taken as a whole, is to consider the impact of current thinking and research on the future provision for these pupils. Are there conclusive arguments in favour of increasing opportunities for the further integration of pupils with learning difficulties? Should we plan to close all special schools and relocate these pupils in mainstream provision? If so how should this provision be organized and resourced to ensure that the pupils receive an inclusive education in which all their needs are met?

In order to address these issues this chapter covers the following areas:

- conceptual issues surrounding the definition of integration and inclusion;
- the arguments for and against the integration of pupils with learning difficulties;
- different ways in which pupils with learning difficulties experience integration.

In the following chapter we shall discuss research on integration and consider the implications for the future provision for pupils with learning difficulties.

According to Hegarty (1993) the whole subject of integration has been one of the key issues in special education for the past twenty-five years. The debate has reflected international interest and concern about the range of provision that is offered to all pupils and adults with disabilities and about the potential dangers of segregated placements for the pupils themselves, their families and the community. Many of the arguments about integration apply to all people who are perceived as being 'different' from the majority of their fellow human beings, for example people with physical and sensory difficulties, and are not restricted to pupils with learning difficulties.

Despite government pronouncements about the need to integrate pupils with SEN into mainstream schools, as far as pupils with learning difficulties are concerned, the vast majority are still educated in segregated special schools. For other pupils with SEN, opportunities for placements in integrated provision have increased over the years, particularly for pupils with visual and hearing difficulties and to a lesser extent for pupils with physical handicaps. Developments for pupils with learning difficulties have been far less extensive although, as we shall see later in this chapter, these pupils are being offered increasing opportunities to mix with their mainstream peers but few LEAs have made co-ordinated moves to relocate all of them into mainstream settings.

DEFINITIONS OF INTEGRATION/INCLUSION

The Warnock Report (DES, 1978) suggested there were three main kinds of integration: locational, social and functional. In locational integration pupils are placed in schools or units which are located within a mainstream campus with no contact between the pupils with SEN and their mainstream peers. In social integration children mix with mainstream pupils for social activities, such as mealtimes and school visits, but for the rest of the time they are segregated from their mainstream peers. In functional integration all pupils, whatever their age and disability, are placed in their local mainstream school in a regular classroom setting with their same-age peers.

In recent years, however, the term 'integration' has been used to describe a much wider variety of educational provision which goes far beyond the three types outlined in the Warnock Report. Hegarty (1991) indicates that this could range from occasional visits by a pupil with a disability to a mainstream school, to full-time placement in such schools. Later in this chapter we will consider in more detail some of the different types of integrated provision which can be offered to pupils with learning difficulties.

Defining integration solely in terms of the provision a pupil receives tells us nothing about the quality of the education which is received in this provision. Are pupils placed in units attached to a mainstream school more 'integrated' than if they were taught in a special school? Jupp (1992a) argues that such units can be just as segregating. Similarly a pupil with SEN placed in a mainstream class may in fact be isolated from the rest of the class and not truly 'integrated' within the group, particularly if he/she works with a support worker in one-to-one sessions for the majority of each day. Integrated placements, therefore, may still leave the pupil 'segregated'.

The term 'inclusion' has now become a more accepted way of describing the extent to which a pupil with SEN is truly 'integrated'. Indeed the pressure group which used to be known as the Centre for Studies on Integrated Education (CSIE) has now substituted the word 'Inclusive' for 'Integrated'. Furthermore the International League of Societies for Persons with Mental Handicap has changed its name to Inclusion International. 'Inclusive education' and 'inclusion', therefore, are terms which are here to stay. Essentially they refer to the extent to which a school or community welcomes every person as a fully inclusive member of the group and values them for the contribution which they make. For integration to be effective the pupils must actively belong to, be welcomed by and participate in a mainstream school and community – that is, they should be fully included. Jordan and Powell (1994) provide a helpful discussion of the arguments about the meaning of the words 'integration' and 'inclusion'.

The challenge for parents and professionals is to ensure that, wherever possible, if pupils with learning difficulties are educated in 'integrated' settings, they are also fully 'included'. As regards pupils with learning difficulties, this is a major challenge. Given the range and extent of their learning problems, in particular pupils with profound and multiple learning difficulties, there are huge problems in providing education which is genuinely inclusive and which also takes account of their individual needs.

ARGUMENTS FOR AND AGAINST THE INTEGRATION OF PUPILS WITH LEARNING DIFFICULTIES

'Socio-political' arguments in favour of integration

Lindsay (1989) suggests that there are two perspectives underpinning arguments in favour of integration – the socio-political and empirical. Socio-political arguments view integration as essentially a matter of human rights. The Centre for Studies on Inclusive Education (CSIE 1989) advocates this view forcibly in their Integration Charter:

> We see the ending of segregation in education as a human rights issue which belongs within equal opportunities policies. Segrega-

tion in education because of disability or learning difficulty is a contravention of human rights as is segregation because of race and gender. The difference is that while sexism and racism are widely recognised as discrimination . . . discrimination on the grounds of disability or learning difficulty is not.

Other writers (see for example Whittaker, 1992; Jupp, 1992b, 1993; Tyne, 1993; Hall, 1996) take a similar view. These authors tend to use strong language to describe special schools and the practices that take place within them. For example they state that their very existence perpetuates a form of educational apartheid; they are sometimes described as ghettos; pupils in special schools are devalued; they are second-class citizens who are discriminated against; they are denied the same opportunities that are offered to their peers in mainstream schools.

There is an implication from these arguments that, by placing pupils in special schools, LEAs may be more concerned with meeting other needs and not the needs of pupils with SEN. For example the needs of mainstream schools are being met as their more trouble-some pupils are removed, the needs of staff in special schools are being met as, by keeping the schools full, they have job security; the financial needs of the LEA and special schools are being met as their budgets are geared towards maintaining special schools – and inte-grated education is more expensive. As mentioned in Chapter 1, this is sometimes referred to as Resource-led Statementing (Farrell, 1989, 1995) where statements are drawn up to meet the needs of the LEA to keep within its existing budget and to help special schools maintain their numbers rather than to meet the needs of the pupils.

As can be observed from the above discussion, socio-political argu-ments about integration are often expressed in language which is challenging and emotive and which may oversimplify the issue. Inte-gration is in fact an extremely complex topic. There are conflicting views among parents and professionals about the desirability of inte-gration and the research evidence is by no means conclusive.

Those who favour a more flexible approach to special school pro-vision for pupils with SEN (see, for example, Segal, 1993; Ouvry, 1994) take issue with the socio-political arguments on a number of counts. One of these concerns the issue of whether special schools devalue pupils and deny them equal opportunities, and another con-cerns the arguments about human rights. Each of these is explored in more detail below.

According to the CSIE, pupils in special schools are devalued and are denied the same opportunities as their mainstream peers. This is a provocative statement which requires some analysis. Any visitor to a special school is likely to find that the pupils seem to be happy, that they experience a rich and stimulating education and that their teachers are keen and enthusiastic and enjoy teaching them. The pupils are offered a range of opportunities which are often far more extensive and challenging than they might experience in a mainstream school. How can such pupils be described as devalued? Do they feel devalued? Do their teachers, peers and parents devalue them? It could be argued that they would feel far more devalued and isolated in a mainstream class surrounded by unsympathetic teachers and pupils. To say that pupils in special schools are devalued and denied equal opportunities is at best simplistic and at worst wholly misleading.

The argument that placing pupils in special schools is a denial of basic human rights should also not go unchallenged. The United Nations Convention has published a booklet on the rights of the pupil (United Nations, 1993). As regards children with disabilities, Article 23 states that 'children should be helped to become as independent as possible and to be able to take a full and active part in everyday life'. Nowhere does it mention that these pupils should be taught in mainstream educational settings and, indeed, the aims of the Article are quite compatible with the notion that pupils with special needs may receive excellent education in special schools. The International League of Societies for Persons with Mental Handicap (Inclusion International) has recently published the Delhi Declaration on the Rights and Needs of Persons with Mental Handicap and their Families (ILSMH, 1994) which also makes no mention of the need to educate pupils with SEN in integrated settings. The views of the CSIE and others therefore appear to be out of step with current thinking on human rights.

The logical extension of their position that placing pupils in special schools represents a denial of human rights is that such schools should all be abolished. Therefore integrated education would be offered to all pupils with SEN. Would this deny parents and pupils the right of self-determination in that they would be denied the right to choose a special school for their pupil? As Lewis (1993, p. 8) has asked,

> which is the more fundamental right: does a right to self-determination over-ride the right to integrated education if the outcome of these two sets of rights come into conflict?

Ouvry (1994) and Segal (1993) are also concerned that parents and pupils should be given the right to choose the provision for their pupils.

The key point about Article 23 of the UN Convention on Human Rights is that societies should do all they can to help pupils with disabilities become as independent as possible so that they can take a full and active part in everyday life. It is possible that high quality integrated education may make this more likely. But this remains an open question and special schools would undoubtedly claim that they are also doing all they can to achieve this aim.

'Empirical' arguments in favour of integration

As the above discussion illustrates, socio-political arguments about integration are contentious. Lindsay (1989) considers that there are also empirical arguments in favour of integration, which, unlike socio-political arguments, can be tested against research evidence. Some of these are discussed below in relation to pupils with learning difficulties.

- *Pupils with learning difficulties model appropriate behaviour from their mainstream peers.* In particular it is argued that in integrated settings pupils with learning difficulties benefit from being in a more language-enriched environment among a peer group whose behaviour is likely to be age-appropriate.
- *In mainstream schools pupils with learning difficulties will have access to a broader curriculum and increased resources.* Because of their size, special schools do not have the equipment and facilities typically found in mainstream schools and, as a result, their curriculum is too narrow and their resources restricted.
- *Placing pupils with learning difficulties in mainstream schools raises parents' and teachers' expectations.* Special schools are also segregating for parents and teachers and this can result in their expectations of what the pupils can do being reduced as opportunities to observe and interact with pupils in mainstream schools is restricted.
- *Parents prefer integration.* One of the key arguments of pressure groups such as the CSIE is that parents are keen for their pupils with learning difficulties to be integrated and that they have felt unduly pressurized to comply with a special school placement when faced with pressure from the array of 'experts'.
- *Integration benefits mainstream pupils and their teachers.* Including pupils with learning difficulties in mainstream schools helps mainstream pupils and adults learn about the problems faced by those with disabilities and their families, and this contributes to society becoming more caring and compassionate. If we segregate, it is argued, we forget about those who could be

described as less fortunate; if we ever meet them, we are afraid, we feel helpless and wish to escape. To be a truly caring society all people with disabilities should live, work and go to school in their local community and should be seen to have a valued role in it. Integration is one important step in this process.

Arguments in favour of segregation

Historically people with similar problems and characteristics have always been placed together, for example prisoners, elderly and mentally ill people. There is also a tendency for those with special talents to be placed together, for example pupils who are musically gifted or highly intelligent. Similarly people with disabilities have traditionally been segregated from their fellow peers. By selecting these people for segregated provision, society has at least recognized that it has a responsibility to provide services. Despite the arguments for integration that have been outlined above, there is a strongly held view that pupils with similar characteristics do learn more effectively if they are educated together. Lubovoski (1988), in an impassioned account, argues strongly in favour of this position.

As regards pupils with learning difficulties, what are the arguments in favour of segregated provision? Some of these are discussed below.

- *The learning difficulties experienced by pupils with learning difficulties are so great that it is unrealistic for them to share the same curriculum as that of their mainstream colleagues.* This argument in favour of segregation does not apply to pupils with visual, hearing or physical difficulties where, with the careful adaptation of teaching materials and with specialized equipment, it is possible for them to work at the same level as their peers. Pupils with learning difficulties, however, are likely to need a curriculum which is differentiated to such an extent that it bears no resemblance to that of their peer group. If this is the case, one has to question the level of integration which actually takes place when a pupil is working on such completely different tasks. This problem becomes more acute for older pupils and for pupils with profound and multiple learning difficulties.
- *The degree of careful planning required to teach pupils with learning difficulties effectively can only be done in special schools.* Not only do pupils with learning difficulties require a highly differentiated curriculum, but a great deal of care and thought has to be given to how to teach it. This will be done more effectively by trained and experienced staff who are less likely to be available if pupils are integrated in mainstream schools throughout the LEA.

- *Specialist resources can be concentrated in one place.* This includes the provision of speech and physiotherapy services and facilities such as adapted toilets and multi-sensory rooms.
- *Teachers choose to teach pupils with learning difficulties.* The vast majority of teachers in schools for pupils with learning difficulties choose to work in such settings and find their work rewarding. In contrast, teachers in mainstream schools, whose classes contain a pupil with learning difficulties, may not have any choice in the placement. They may be completely ignorant about the needs of such pupils and have no desire to teach them. They may also feel uncomfortable working alongside a support worker. This understandable reluctance may well affect the success of the integration.
- *It is easier to establish parent support groups in segregated settings.* It is well known that parents of pupils with learning difficulties value meeting other parents of similar pupils in order to share experiences and concerns. It is easier to establish parent groups if the pupils all go to the same school.
- *Pupils are in a peer group which is likely to be the same age and ability.* A pupil with learning difficulties in a mainstream class will almost certainly be the least able member of the group. This may affect his/her self-esteem and self-confidence. In a special school he/she will be with peers of a similar ability and, as a result, it is easier to interact in a way which is enjoyable and meaningful even though it may not be age-appropriate. It is difficult for pupils with learning difficulties to engage in reciprocal play at a level which is genuinely interactive if their peer group consists of pupils who are much more able than they are.
- *It is safer in special schools.* Special schools are smaller and better staffed than mainstream schools and therefore pupils with learning difficulties, many of whom may have additional physical and sensory problems, are less likely to be at risk from large numbers of unruly pupils in a mainstream setting than they are in a special school.
- *It is more economical to teach pupils with learning difficulties in special schools.* Debates about integration often come down to this crucial point. According to the HMI/Audit Commission Report (1992) it costs about £7,500 to educate a pupil with severe learning difficulties in a day special school. It is often argued that, to be successfully integrated in a mainstream class, a pupil with learning difficulties requires the services of a support worker, possibly full-time, and back-up support from an experienced teacher of pupils with learning difficulties who visits on a weekly basis. This level of support costs the LEA more than it does to educate a

pupil in a school for pupils with learning difficulties. However, if all special schools were to close down then LEAs would make a saving and, as a result, the arguments about cost become more finely balanced.

Summary of the arguments for and against the integration of pupils with learning difficulties

The socio-political arguments in favour of integration tend to be laced with emotive rhetoric about human rights. They can give the impression that, by definition, segregation is always bad and, as a result, the real achievements which have been made in special schools are not acknowledged. Empirical arguments in favour of integration suggest that there may be real social, linguistic and behavioural benefits from integration and that pupils and teachers in mainstream schools will also benefit. Arguments in favour of special schools focus on the very real problems of realistically meeting the curricular needs of pupils with learning difficulties in a mainstream school and on the problems of allocating sufficient resources to the mainstream context.

WAYS OF INTEGRATING PUPILS WITH LEARNING DIFFICULTIES

The previous section on the arguments for and against the integration of pupils with learning difficulties did not distinguish between the different types of integration which pupils can experience. There is in fact a wide variety of provision which is described as 'integrated'. It is therefore important, when discussing the potential benefits of integrated provision, to be absolutely clear about the type of integration which is under discussion. In this section a number of examples of different types of provision for pupils with learning difficulties is discussed each of which brings these pupils into contact with a more able peer group and could therefore be described as 'integrated'.

1. Full-time placement in a local neighbourhood school.
This is equivalent to functional integration as originally described in the Warnock Report. Pupils with learning difficulties attend their local mainstream school, in a same age group throughout their school life, with support services being brought into the school. This would apply to all pupils with learning difficulties no matter how severe their disability.

At the present time there are no LEAs which have adopted this wholesale policy of functionally integrating all pupils with learning difficulties. However there are increasing examples of LEAs offering this level of integration to infant and junior-age pupils with Down's Syndrome. Other more able pupils with learning difficulties may also be placed in mainstream schools. Anecdotal evidence suggests that many parents have had to fight to obtain this provision and that there are few LEAs who have allocated sufficient resources to support mainstream provision for all pupils whose parents request it. Leeds is one LEA which has gone some way to taking this step as it places between 67 per cent and 81 per cent of pupils with Down's Syndrome in infant schools although the number declines somewhat as the pupils get older (Lorenz, 1995). Moorcroft-Cuckle (1993) also found a gradual increase in the initial placement of pupils with Down's Syndrome into mainstream schools. Her sample was gathered from eleven Local Authority Special Needs registers. A further survey of twenty-three LEAs (Wyton, 1993) revealed that thirteen did not functionally integrate any of its pupils with learning difficulties and that only four integrated more than six such pupils.

On the whole, therefore, functional integration, as defined here, is only offered to more able pupils with learning difficulties, in particular pupils with Down's Syndrome, and there are many LEAs which are still reluctant to integrate any of their pupils with learning difficulties. Integration, when it does occur, is likely to be for younger pupils and only a few are integrated into secondary schools. Typically LEAs employ additional staff on a full- or half-time basis, usually qualified nursery nurses or unqualified teaching assistants, to support the pupil with learning difficulties in the mainstream class. These support staff may receive the advice and guidance of a teacher from a local special school but, apart from the Leeds initiative (Lorenz 1995), there is little evidence of them receiving systematic training for this role although training materials are available (see, for example, Balshaw, 1991).

2. *Full-time placement in a unit for pupils for learning difficulties housed within a mainstream school.*
This is equivalent to locational integration as described in the Warnock Report. However, if the pupils spend all their time in the unit and never meet their mainstream peers, then it is difficult to describe this provision as being inclusive in any way. Nevertheless, there are a few examples which suggest that this unit model of integration has the potential to offer genuine opportunities for more inclusive provision. Stockport LEA have recently decided to establish four resourced primary schools each of which has a class base for about eight pupils with learning difficulties who are given opportunities to integrate with the rest of the school in accordance with their

individual programme plan. Pupils with profound and multiple learning difficulties are placed in a special school for pupils with physical disabilities. Another well-known example of unit model provision for pupils with learning difficulties is at Bishopswood School in Oxfordshire (*Times Educational Supplement*, 1992) where all the pupils, including those with PMLD, are placed in special classes in a primary and secondary school, both of which are close to the original special school.

Although similar 'unit' models of integration have existed for many years in some rural areas of the country, there is little evidence of a wholesale move towards this type of integration.

3. *The placement of a whole class from a school for pupils with learning difficulties within a mainstream school.*
In this 'model' of integration, a special school links with a local mainstream school and arranges for one of its classes to transfer to the school. Indeed this was how the integrated provision at Bishopswood began. There are a few isolated examples where this type of provision has been arranged although it is too early to say whether it will lead to more radical developments along the lines of Bishopswood.

4. *Full-time placement of students with learning difficulties in a unit based in a college of further education.*
Increasingly, colleges of further education are offering courses to more able students with learning difficulties when they leave school. These students are usually taught in a separate room but they can be given opportunities to integrate with students in the rest of the college, particularly for leisure activities and mealtimes.

5. *Integrated nursery in a school for pupils with severe learning difficulties.*
In this model of integration an SLD school opens its nursery to pupils from the local community who do not have learning difficulties, sometimes referred to as 'playgroup' pupils. Typically these nursery classes contain about eighteen pupils, around half of whom have severe learning difficulties. When the playgroup pupils reach school age, they go to their local mainstream school. This model of integration is unusual as there is a 50/50 balance between pupils with learning difficulties and their more able peers.

6. *Regular visits from pupils in an SLD school into a mainstream school.*
This is perhaps the most common way in which pupils with learning difficulties experience opportunities to mix with their mainstream

peers. Over the past ten years there has been a growth in the number of schools for pupils with severe learning difficulties which have established informal links with local mainstream schools. This enables groups of pupils to visit mainstream schools on a regular basis, usually to join in a leisure activity. Jowett *et al* (1988) found that well over 50 per cent of SLD schools had established such links. In a follow-up study Fletcher-Campbell (1994) found that this number had increased to 70 per cent. The pupils are usually supported by staff from the special school who also arrange the transport. Hence the arrangements are essentially informal and do not require the LEA to increase its expenditure. For some pupils these visits can be extended and may eventually lead to the full-time placement of a pupil in a mainstream school.

7. *Pupils from a local mainstream school visit the special school.*
At best this could only be described as an extremely mild form of integration. Through making these visits both groups of pupils do achieve some contact with each other although it is usually so minimal as to be of doubtful long-term value.

8. *Full- or part-time placement of a pupil in a school for pupils with physical difficulties.*
Again it is difficult to describe this as integration as the pupils with learning difficulties still attend a special school. However they do gain opportunities to mix with a more able peer group and might therefore gain access to an increasingly stretching curriculum.

9. *Pupils with PMLD are 'integrated' into the classes of the SLD school.*
In all the literature on integration the needs of pupils with PMLD tend to be overlooked. If a special school is seriously concerned about integrating its pupils into mainstream schools, then it hardly seems logical for it to maintain a separate special class, within the SLD school, for pupils with PMLD. However, many SLD schools do have such classes. It could be argued that an essential first step towards integration is to abandon PMLD classes and integrate the pupils within the remainder of the special school. An increasing number of schools are now organized in this way although some have adopted a flexible model, having a resource base for pupils with PMLD with regular opportunities for the pupils to join in activities with the rest of the school. O'Connell (1994) provides an interesting account of a small-scale study of the integration of two pupils with PMLD into a regular class in a learning difficulties school. His study suggests that,

without careful preparation and support, the tangible gains from such integration are in fact quite minimal.

This chapter has shown that there are many ways in which pupils with learning difficulties can experience 'integration' and that these may be quite different from each other. When discussing integration with parents and professional colleagues and when evaluating research findings, it is important to be clear about the level of integration which is being discussed. The types of integration which have attracted the most publicity are full neighbourhood integration into a mainstream class and the unit model. However, the most common form of integration emanates from regular links between special and mainstream schools. Overall it is important to remember that, despite initiatives towards integration which are taking place, the vast majority of pupils with learning difficulties are still educated in special schools throughout their school life.

CONCLUSION

Integration is a complex topic. There are many people with strongly held views and this often leads to debates about the subject becoming extremely heated. This chapter has attempted to take a dispassionate and objective view of the issues surrounding the integration of pupils with learning difficulties. We have considered the definition of the terms 'integration' and 'inclusion' and have reviewed some of the arguments for and against integration. The range of provision which is offered to pupils with learning difficulties in the name of integration only serves to illustrate the huge breadth of integrated experiences which are 'on offer'. In the following chapter some of the research evidence on the effectiveness of integration will be considered and a range of options for the development of more inclusive provision will be discussed.

CHAPTER 10

Research on integration: implications for future provision

INTRODUCTION

When discussing prospects for the integration of pupils with severe learning difficulties, a natural question to ask is 'Is integration effective?' Unfortunately this apparently simple question is by no means easy to answer. In research into any aspect of education, it has consistently proved difficult to establish firm and unequivocal conclusions. For example, there have been countless studies evaluating different approaches to teaching reading, yet academics and teachers still do not know which is the best approach. It is perhaps because of the lack of hard data that policies in the field of education tend to be made on the basis of socio-political beliefs. As there is a wide diversity of professional opinions in the area of education, it is usually possible for politicians to seek advice from 'academics' who support their view, not because of conclusive research evidence, but because they, too, in the final analysis are driven by their socio-political ideology. In this climate, sound theory and research-led advice to policy-makers is noticeable by its absence.

In the area of integration, socio-political ideologies laced with emotive rhetoric have been particularly evident in the many books and articles which have been written about the subject. Whether these or pragmatic considerations have been most influential in shaping policy and provision is an open question. Our task in this chapter, however, is to review the research on integration that has taken place and to consider how this should inform future policy and provision.

METHODOLOGICAL ISSUES IN EVALUATING INTEGRATION

As implied above, reviewing research on integration is not an easy task because of the intractable methodological problems which make it difficult to arrive at firm conclusions about the effects of integration. These problems affect the quality of evaluative studies on the integration of all types of pupils with SEN, including those with learning difficulties. Madden and Slavin (1983), Danby and Cullen (1988) and Hegarty (1993) provide an extensive review of the issues. Some of the main ones are discussed below.

- When evaluating the effectiveness of integrated provision it is virtually impossible to use matched control group designs where one group of pupils is placed in integrated provision and another is placed in a special school. This is because of the ethical problems involved in allocating different provision to similar pupils for research purposes only and to problems in matching accurately pupils with SEN so as to be certain that the two groups have the same characteristics.
- The range of problems evident in pupils with disabilities is so great that it is difficult to generalize from one study to another unless one can be absolutely sure that the studies that are being compared were conducted on similar pupils. As Lewis (1995) points out, 'it is not clear whether, for example pupils designated "trainable mentally retarded" (USA), having "moderate learning difficulties", (Australia and New Zealand) or "severe learning difficulties" (UK) represent similar groups' (p. 10).
- Similarly, the variety of integrated provision which pupils can experience is so great that it is difficult to compare the findings from different studies as it is not always easy to judge whether the groups experienced similar or entirely different forms of integration.
- It is possible, though hard to verify objectively, that researchers may have a vested interest in showing that their integration scheme is effective and that therefore they only report on results which support their preconceived views.

Despite the considerable methodological problems inherent in evaluating integration, there is no shortage of literature on the subject. Essentially there are four different kinds of studies which have attempted to evaluate integration. First, there are anecdotal accounts from schools, parents and professionals of a particular integration experience. Second, there are a number of detailed case studies of pupils or schools which provide data on a range of factors connected with an integration scheme. Third, there are a small number of longitudinal studies of cohorts of pupils with a range of different SEN, some of which have attempted to use control groups, whose progress is monitored over a period of time. Fourth, there are a number of attitude surveys which have sought the views of parents, teachers and other professionals about integration.

This chapter reviews some recent research into the integration of pupils with learning difficulties and updates earlier reviews by Farrell and Sugden (1985) and Mittler and Farrell (1987). An excellent overall review is also provided by Jenkinson (1993) who comments on the paucity of research aimed specifically at the integration of this group of pupils.

The review is divided into the following sections:

1. The role of support workers and their impact on integration.
2. The effect of integration on linguistic interaction.
3. The relevance of curriculum differentiation.
4. The impact of the age, ability and behaviour of the pupils with learning difficulties on the success of integration.
5. The effects of integration on pupils without learning difficulties.
6. The attitudes of mainstream teachers and LEA staff towards integration.

THE ROLE OF SUPPORT WORKERS AND THEIR IMPACT ON INTEGRATION

General issues

One of the key factors which has been associated with the success of integration is the availability and adequacy of in-class support workers. For example Center *et al* (1991), in a two-year study of the integration of pupils with disabilities into regular classrooms – of whom thirty-five had 'intellectual disabilities', found that the availability of appropriate resource support to be central to the success of integration. Appropriate resource support was defined in terms of the training and professional supervision which the support worker received, the extent to which they were able to use team teaching approaches and whether their teaching was appropriate to the pupil's needs. The OECD/CERI project (1992), which reported on seven case studies of integration in the United Kingdom, also stressed the key role played by support staff, a view strongly supported by Balshaw (1991), Jones (1994), Murphy (1994) and Gregory (1996). Although many of the pupils featured in the above studies did not have learning difficulties, there is every reason to believe that the support teacher/worker's role is also crucial to the successful integration of these pupils.

The role of support workers in planning and teaching individual programmes

A further factor associated with the success of integration is the extent to which systematic and structured teaching techniques are used within the integrated context. Studies by Center (*op. cit.*), Philps (1994) and reviews of the evidence (Jenkinson, 1993; Zigler *et al*, 1990) all make this point. This help should be offered by trained support staff working in collaboration with the mainstream teacher and with support from senior colleagues. The challenge is for the staff to ensure that pupils with learning difficulties receive sufficient systematic and structured teaching while at the same time remaining an integrated part of the group. Philps (*op. cit.*), for example, considers that some of the pupils in her sample made good 'academic' progress at the expense of giving them opportunities to experience greater social interaction with their mainstream peers. In addition, Rouse and Florin (1996), in their study of inclusion in the London borough of Newham, concluded that there was a risk that the teaching of structured individually tailored programmes could prevent pupils with SEN from being fully included within the classroom.

The role of the support worker in encouraging social interaction

One of the main arguments for integration is that it facilitates social interaction between the mainstream pupils and their peers with learning difficulties. Evidence in support of this argument is inconclusive (see Conway and Baker, 1996, for an up-to-date review of the issues). In a special school nursery class containing eight pupils with severe learning difficulties and eight pupils who did not have any disabilities (playgroup pupils) Farrell and Scales (1995) found that pupils in the learning difficulties group were equally likely to choose to play with and sit next to pupils from either group. The playgroup pupils, however, showed a slight preference for their own group. Vizziello *et al* (1994) obtained similar results in a study of the social interaction between mainstream and autistic pupils. In Ware *et al*'s (1992) study, however, where there were only a few pupils with learning difficulties in a range of different integrated settings, they found that there was limited interaction between the pupils but there was also limited interaction in special schools as well. In a similar study, Lewis (1995) found that mainstream pupils tended to dominate the activities in the integrated settings in a way which encouraged pupils with learning difficulties to take on a more passive role. Her evidence suggests that there is an increased chance of social interaction occurring if the pupils with learning difficulties work on activities with which they are familiar and which are novel to the mainstream pupils and if the groups are more closely matched by developmental level, e.g. if 7-year-old mainstream pupils are placed with 10-year-old pupils with learning difficulties. However she acknowledges that this may be controversial on social and emotional grounds if the difference in chronological age is too great.

Stobart (1986), Frederickson and Wolfson (1987) and Jenkinson (1993) conclude that social interaction does not simply occur by placing pupils with disabilities with their mainstream peers: it needs to be fostered and encouraged. Pedlar (1990), when studying the integration of young adults with disabilities into community settings, suggests that the support staff might have been hindering social interaction by adopting an over-protective attitude towards their clients. Lewis (1995) also found that the support worker's involvement could impede social interaction. Slee (1991), Philps (1994) and Lincoln *et al* (1992) also argue that, by devoting too much time to one-to-one teaching, support workers, far from facilitating social interaction, may act as a barrier to prevent it. Without the presence of support workers, integration will most certainly fail; but their very presence may prevent the occurrence of the social integration which is being sought.

In separate studies Hundert and Houghton (1992) and Sainato *et al* (1992) have tried to overcome this problem by using the support worker to train mainstream pupils to interact positively with integrated pupils with disabilities. In both studies the level of social interaction improved but there were problems with maintenance over time and generalization across settings. The problem is highlighted by Stainback *et al* (1994) who refer to the dangers of artificially structuring social interaction, as such behaviour occurs more naturally when participants are given a free choice and are not 'forced' to mix with pupils with disabilities. Ware *et al* (1992) suggest that team teaching and co-operative learning are necessary to achieve this end. Pupils should share in the experiences of their mainstream colleagues and should not just be placed alongside them (Steele and Mitchell, 1992). The support worker should adopt the role of being a 'detached but vigilant observer' (Lewis, 1995).

The role of support workers is therefore one of the keys to successful social integration. However, the precise role that they play can have an effect on the degree to which the pupils are actually 'included'. Hegarty (1987) is perhaps being optimistic when he suggests that friendships can be facilitated by sensitive staff 'setting up conditions which encourage constructive interactions and foster the growth of friendships'. At the present time the evidence suggests that, for pupils with learning difficulties, this is extremely hard to do.

The relationship between support staff and class teachers

According to Jones (1994), Thomas (1992), Sebba and Ainscow (1996b), Evans (1995) and Rouse and Florian (1996) the relationship between the class teacher and the support worker is crucial to the success of integration. To work effectively they have to operate as a team where respective roles are agreed upon in a planned and rational manner so that the needs of all the pupils are met. This requires the staff to be open and honest in their communication with each other, to acknowledge their respective strengths and weaknesses and to be prepared to be flexible by, for example, adapting teaching styles, classroom seating arrangements and the curriculum. This may be difficult to achieve if a class teacher in the mainstream school feels under pressure to accept a pupil with learning difficulties and if the support worker is inexperienced and untrained. Lopez (1994), for example, found that, as a result of poor communication between support staff and class teachers, support staff felt isolated and this affected the success of the integration.

The need for training support workers

It is clear from the discussion so far that, to be a successful support worker, it is necessary to be able to plan and carry out individual programmes which are tailored to the needs of the pupil while at the same time working collaboratively with other staff and pupils so as to facilitate maximum social interaction between the pupil with learning difficulties and his/her mainstream peers. To fulfil this role adequately, support workers require ongoing training and support. Many such staff are not qualified teachers and they may have had no prior experience of working with pupils with learning difficulties. Some form of training is therefore crucial in order for them to fulfil their role effectively, a point made by Rouse and Florian (1996), Howlin (1994) and many others. Lorenz (1994) describes the training offered to support staff in Leeds and suggests that it needs to be skills-based as well as incorporating whole school approaches advocated by Balshaw (1991). Mortimer (1995) has also developed a range of practical strategies aimed at preparing support staff and teachers to include infant-age pupils with disabilities in their mainstream classes. However, over the UK as a whole, there is a lack of systematic and ongoing training offered to support staff and this can have an adverse effect on the success of integration schemes (Spencer 1993). An alternative view is suggested by Jupp (1992b) who argues that, by offering specialist training to support staff, we are running the risk of segregating them from their colleagues as they will be seen as having specific skills which no other staff have. If they are seen as being different from their colleagues in view of their specialist training, this may reinforce the general perception that the pupils for whom they are responsible for are also 'different'.

THE EFFECT OF INTEGRATION ON COMMUNICATION AND LINGUISTIC INTERACTION

Problems in fostering social interaction are inexorably linked to the issue of whether the experience of integration increases the quality of the language and communication used by pupils with learning difficulties. On the whole, research suggests that quality of discourse in integrated settings is somewhat one-sided. Bayliss (1995) has found that communication between mainstream pupils and those with learning difficulties tends to be didactic and that this actually prevents the pupils with learning difficulties from developing and enhancing their own language as they tend to be asked to respond to 'demands' and not to 'interact' verbally. Indeed he found that the 'quality' of language was better in special schools where the level of linguistic interaction between the pupils was more 'equal'. 'Directive' interactional styles observed by Bayliss are, according to Mirenda and Donnellan (1986), less successful than 'facilitative' styles in encouraging initiations and spontaneous language from students with disabilities. This suggests that, in order for pupils with learning difficulties to develop spontaneous and interactive language, they should not be integrated into mainstream classes, especially if they are the only pupils with learning difficulties in the class. However, Lewis (1995) has accumulated anecdotal evidence which suggests that pupils with learning difficulties can repeat language that they have heard from mainstream pupils in appropriate contexts on different occasions and that therefore, although the interaction in the mainstream class may be didactic, the pupils with learning difficulties have benefited. Casey *et al* (1988) also found that pupils with Down's Syndrome, placed in integrated settings, made small but significant gains in language comprehension when compared with pupils with Down's Syndrome educated in special schools. However Howlin (1994) points out that these pupils were comparatively able and she also quotes research to suggest that the success of integration in fostering developments in language and cognition is highly dependent on the pupils' cognitive levels.

THE RELEVANCE OF CURRICULUM DIFFERENTIATION

As we have discussed in Chapter 6, the advent of the National Curriculum has brought a shift in emphasis in curriculum development for pupils with learning difficulties. It has been argued that the more similarities there are between the curriculum in mainstream and special schools, the easier it will be to integrate. This may work effectively for pupils with physical and sensory disabilities but it is difficult for the curriculum for pupils with learning difficulties, however differentiated, to resemble the National Curriculum in a meaningful way. Jordan and Powell (1994), when reporting on the results of their case studies, strongly reject the relevance of a 'Curriculum for All' and prefer instead the phrase 'Curriculum Principles for All'. Indeed, a curriculum which has been substantially differentiated is potentially segregating as the pupils will be working on completely different activities which can have the effect of highlighting the differences between them and their mainstream peers. This has to be carefully considered when weighing up the pros and cons of integrated education. Despite the excellent and innovative work on curriculum development referred to in Chapter 6, there is little or no evidence to suggest that this has had any direct bearing on developments towards more inclusive education for pupils with learning difficulties in mainstream settings. Indeed, as Halpin and Lewis (1996) indicate, despite the notion of promoting curricular integration through the National Curriculum, there has been little impact on the amount of integration which is actually taking place.

THE IMPACT OF THE AGE, ABILITY AND BEHAVIOUR OF PUPILS WITH LEARNING DIFFICULTIES ON THE SUCCESS OF INTEGRATION

A consistent theme running through the research on the impact of integration on pupils with learning difficulties, is that integration tends to be more effective if it is started at nursery school, if the pupils are more able and if they do not present challenging behaviour. This is confirmed by Center *et al* (1991), Cole *et al* (1992), Howlin (1994) and in the review by Jenkinson (1993). None of these findings is all that surprising although they do have implications for the planning of integrated services. Booth (1996) and Beveridge (1996), however, do report some encouraging findings from their research into the integration of secondary-age pupils with learning difficulties.

THE EFFECTS OF INTEGRATION ON PUPILS WITHOUT LEARNING DIFFICULTIES

In addition to bringing benefits to pupils with learning difficulties, a further aim of integration is to help *all* pupils to learn about the lives of pupils with disabilities. In this way it may be possible to begin to break down some of the myths and prejudices that exist in the minds of many people concerning pupils with learning difficulties and, as a result, society as a whole will develop a more inclusive attitude. Carpenter (1994), for example, stresses the importance of helping mainstream pupils to develop positive attitudes towards pupils with disabilities, arguing strongly that this is one of the keys to successful integration and he stresses the vital role that schools should play in this process. Lewis (1990, 1995) reports on ways in which teachers can achieve this objective.

On the whole the evidence suggests that pupils without disabilities do adopt an accepting attitude towards their integrated colleagues and there are a number of anecdotal accounts which support this view (see for example Carson, 1992). This finding is supported by the results from empirical studies. Whittaker (1994), for example, found that 70 per cent of a sample of ninety secondary-age pupils had positive views about the integration of eleven pupils with learning difficulties. Scales (1993) compared the attitudes of 7-year-old pupils who had attended an integrated nursery two years earlier with the attitude of a similar group of pupils who had not had this experience. She found that the attitudes of the group which had been exposed to pupils with disabilities were far more positive than those who had not. In an unpublished study the author has assessed the attitudes of three groups of 7-year-old pupils, each of which had experienced different levels of exposure to pupils with Down's Syndrome. The results showed that pupils who had experienced the greatest level of exposure had the most positive attitudes and those with no experience were most negative. Girls were also more positive than boys. Hastings and Graham (1995) obtained similar results when studying adolescents' attitudes towards pupils with severe learning difficulties. Those who had experienced most contact with such pupils expressed more positive views about the prospect of meeting similar pupils than those who had limited contact. Once again the attitude of girls was more positive than boys. Beveridge (1996) studied the attitudes of secondary-age pupils in one comprehensive school which had set up a link scheme with a local SLD school. On the whole the pupils were very positive about the scheme, many felt they had developed good relationships with the pupils with learning difficulties and that they would benefit from further functional integration into less academic subjects such as drama, music and art. In a longitudinal study Vizziello *et al* (1994) found that, after a ten-year gap, pupils who had been educated alongside pupils with disabilities tended to obtain jobs in the helping professions in a greater proportion than is usual for Italy.

Although mainstream pupils generally have positive and accepting attitudes towards pupils with learning difficulties, as we have seen from the earlier discussion on social interaction, it appears that they have difficulty forming friendships and that the level of interaction tends to be 'one way', with the mainstream pupil leading and the pupil with learning difficulties following. Although 75 per cent of the mainstream pupils with most contact with the 'learning difficulties' group in Beveridge's study did say that they were 'friends', they acknowledged that the level of friendship was different than that which they experience with their mainstream colleagues. Perhaps this is not a surprising finding as the essence of friendship is of a two-way mutual interchange of values and ideas and of a sharing of interests and experiences. It would be difficult to conceive of genuine friendships, defined in this way, being formed between people whose abilities are so different. Indeed one mainstream pupil in Beveridge's study said 'You couldn't tell them secrets and things like that.'

THE ATTITUDE OF MAINSTREAM TEACHERS AND LEA STAFF TOWARDS INTEGRATION

According to Center *et al* (1991), Hanline and Halvorsen (1989), Jenkinson (1993), Murphy (1994), Lewis (1995), Sebba and Ainscow (1996b) and many others, one of the major factors associated with the success of integration is the level of support and commitment from the staff in the mainstream school, the local authority and the community. If they are fully behind the integration scheme, have been involved in the planning and preparation and are willing to work co-operatively with the support staff, then there is a good chance that the integration will be successful.

This level of support and commitment is possible when everyone involved has a positive attitude towards integration. Indeed, Westwood (1993) points out that developments towards greater integration were based on the assumption that teachers would have a positive attitude towards accepting pupils with disabilities into their classes. However, two recent Australian studies (Ward *et al*, 1994; Forlin, 1995) have both cast doubt on the validity of this assumption. Ward and his colleagues conducted a large-scale survey of the attitudes towards integration of headteachers, support teachers, teachers, local authority administrators and school psychologists.

In general the findings were mixed with those staff who were the furthest removed from the classroom, i.e. administrators and psychologists, having the most positive attitudes with staff who might have most contact with the pupils with SEN, the class teachers, being the most negative. In general, attitudes towards integration were most negative for pupils with the most severe disabilities. There was also concern about the need to provide adequate resourcing to support integration. The conclusion from Forlin's study of the attitudes of 273 teachers were that they felt that integration was not suitable for all pupils with SEN and that, as in Ward *et al*'s study, the more severe the disability, the more negative the attitudes. Experienced teachers also had more negative attitudes than those who were newly qualified. Those teachers who worked with pupils with SEN found it to be more stressful than they expected, although headteachers reported a reduction in stress levels having integrated one or more pupils with disabilities. Support service staff did not experience the same level of stress as the class teachers.

One theme emerging from both these studies is that those who have day-to-day responsibility for working with integrated pupils tend to feel the most apprehensive, and moreover, as Forlin stresses, they tend to have no choice as to whether or not a pupil with SEN will be placed in their class. Indeed Phillips and McCulloch (1990) argue that class teachers should have the right to refuse to take a pupil with SEN. Without this protection being offered, the class teacher can be placed in a potentially powerless and vulnerable position. There are clear implications from Ward *et al*'s and Forlin's work, concerning the level of support and training which should be offered to mainstream class teachers, if integration is to be successful.

Other studies on teachers' attitudes towards integrating pupils with learning difficulties have yielded more optimistic findings. For example Toon (1988) found that the staff involved in ten British integration schemes were extremely positive about the overall benefits to the pupils with learning difficulties and their peers. This is also reflected in Rouse and Florian's (1996) review of integration in Newham. Furthermore a recent study by Hastings *et al* (in press) showed that the attitudes of student teachers towards pupils with severe learning difficulties were more positive if they had had previous contact with such pupils and that lectures they received on the topic were not in themselves sufficient to bring about a change in attitude.

SUMMARY OF RESEARCH EVIDENCE

The following observations are intended to summarize the main conclusions concerning research on the integration of pupils with learning difficulties.

1. The complex methodological issues involved and the variability in quality of the studies make it extremely difficult to compare the results of one study with another. In addition many studies focus on the integration of pupils with a range of disabilities and, even if they focus on pupils with learning difficulties, it is not always easy to ascertain if they are referring to those whom, in the UK, would be described as having learning difficulties. In addition the range of integrated provision being evaluated varies from study to study resulting in further problems in making comparisons between them.

2. Notwithstanding these methodological concerns, the vast majority of studies report that pupils in mainstream schools accept their peers with disabilities and do not chastise or reject them.

3. For integration to be successful it is vital for teachers, managers, local authority personnel, parents and pupils to be wholly committed.

4. Mainstream and advisory teachers require training and support.

5. Integration is more common and successful for younger pupils.

6. Pupils with learning difficulties require structured, carefully planned and differentiated teaching programmes.

7. The degree of social and linguistic interaction between the pupils with learning difficulties and their peers is limited and tends to be didactic in nature.

8. The attitudes of teachers in mainstream schools, in particular those who do not have a pupil with learning difficulties in their class, are by no means uniformly positive. The more handicapped the pupil the more negative the attitudes appear to be.

9. Finally the role of support staff is both complex and crucial. That pupils with learning difficulties should be supported adequately by appropriately trained staff is not in question. However research suggests that if support workers devote their time to the delivery of a carefully planned individual programme which undoubtedly helps the pupils to learn basic skills, opportunities for social interaction with their peer group become reduced and the very act of teaching a pupil with learning difficulties individually in a corner of the mainstream class may be viewed as segregation by all those involved, including the pupils. However, if the support worker devotes time to fostering social interaction, this may leave less

time for individual teaching. Furthermore it is by no means an easy task to foster social interaction between the pupils. If the pupil with learning difficulties is simply placed with a group of mainstream pupils, he/she may be ignored; if the support worker joins in, this can influence the 'naturalness' of the interaction.

FUTURE PROVISION FOR PUPILS WITH LEARN-ING DIFFICULTIES: THREE POSSIBLE OPTIONS

Although the majority of pupils with learning difficulties still go to special schools, there is an increasing number of accounts of schools developing local initiatives to extend opportunities for integration. Many of these have begun as a result of pressure from individual parents who did not want their pupil to go to a special school. As we have seen, there are only a few accounts of LEAs as a whole taking the initiative and, as a result, reorganizing their provision for these pupils. In view of these developments and the associated research findings, it is legitimate to ask more fundamental questions about the long-term future provision for pupils with learning difficulties. Have we reached the stage where there is sufficient evidence from research and a substantial commitment from parents and professionals to indicate that large-scale changes in provision for pupils with learning difficulties should now be implemented? Is it sensible to continue to proceed towards increased integration through locally developed initiatives which exist at present? If these initiatives continue to develop and expand, the continued existence of special schools will be called into question. Indeed, is there a future for special schools anyway? Is it possible to conceive of a model of educational provision for pupils with learning difficulties which is integrated and inclusive, where pupils' needs are met and which is adequately resourced?

In the remainder of this chapter we will consider three contrasting options for the long-term future educational provision for pupils with learning difficulties and discuss the arguments for and against them in the light of current trends in special needs provision and the research evidence. These options are neighbourhood integration, special schools with outreach and special units in mainstream schools.

Option 1: Neighbourhood integration

This is equivalent to functional integration as defined by the Warnock Report. All pupils, regardless of their disability, would go to their local school where additional support and resources would be provided. Such placements already exist for a number of primary-age pupils with learning difficulties but they are extremely rare in secondary schools.

Although there are many arguments in favour of this type of provision which are explored in the previous chapter, and some evidence that younger pupils with learning difficulties do benefit, there are a number of concerns which suggest that it may not be suitable for a great many pupils with learning difficulties. First, as pupils get older, the gap in attainments and curricular needs between those with learning difficulties and their mainstream peers becomes increasingly large. This means that the curriculum has to be even more differentiated to the extent that the pupils are rarely doing similar work. This may inevitably result in pupils with learning difficulties being segregated within the mainstream school. Second, the difficulties in fostering social interaction are more acute for older and more disabled pupils. Third, there is some evidence (Blacher and Turnbull, 1982) that parents of pupils with learning difficulties can feel isolated if their pupil attends the local school as they have less in common with other parents with whom it is difficult to share the experience of bringing up a child with a disability. Fourth, it is difficult to see how pupils with profound and multiple learning difficulties would benefit from neighbourhood integration as their curricular needs are so different from their peer group. If these pupils are excluded from neighbourhood integration, where should they be educated? Is it educationally sensible for them to remain as a separate group in a special school containing, for example, pupils with physical disabilities? Finally the cost of neighbourhood integration, if adequately supported and resourced, is likely to be far in excess of the cost of placing pupils in special schools.

For an increasing number of pupils neighbourhood integration may be an effective option, particularly if it is started at an early age. However, as an option for all pupils with learning difficulties, including those with PMLD, it is probably not viable.

Option 2: Special schools with outreach

This is the most common form of integration as Jowett *et al* (1988) and Fletcher-Campbell (1994) have indicated. Virtually all special schools for pupils with learning difficulties have developed contacts with local mainstream schools which enable many of their pupils to experience opportunities to interact with their mainstream peers. Indeed some special schools have appointed additional staff to fulfil this role. This is, however, the least radical form of integration, and indeed to call it 'integration' could be described as a gross exaggeration. There are obvious advantages for special schools as their continued existence, far from being threatened, is guaranteed and their role is greatly enhanced to that of a resource centre which has the potential to offer support and advice across the mainstream sector. Properly resourced, this option could offer increasingly extended opportunities for pupils with learning difficulties to experience a more inclusive education in mainstream schools from the 'protective' base of the special school. However, if it is resourced sufficiently to allow many pupils to experience considerable periods of time in mainstream schools, the option becomes expensive as two systems start to operate.

Option 3: Units in mainstream schools

In two earlier articles (Farrell and Sugden, 1985; Mittler and Farrell, 1987) a unit model of integrating pupils with learning difficulties has been proposed as providing the best opportunity for these pupils to experience the full benefits of integration while at the same time ensuring that their educational needs are met. This model is summarized in Table 10.1.

It is important to point out that the unit model of integration is not a new idea and already exists in some parts of the country, Bishopswood School being the best-known example (*Times Educational Supplement*, 1992). There are a few other examples of similar initiatives being developed (e.g. in Stockport) but overall progress has been slow.

Under this unit model it is assumed that the whole population of a school for pupils with learning difficulties, including those with PMLD, would be relocated into two primary schools, one secondary school and one further education college. There would be a total of

School	Pupils	Units	Teachers	Assistants
Primary	20	2	3	4
Primary	20	2	3	4
Secondary	30	3	4	6
FE college	10	1	1.5	1
			+2 Sen Ts	
			1 Dep HT	
			1 HT	
Total	80	8	15.5	15

Table 10.1: Unit model of integration in mainstream schools (taken from Mittler and Farrell, 1987)

eight units, with a notional ten pupils per unit, with two units in each of the primary schools, three in the secondary school and one in the FE college. Although the model represented in Table 10.1 assumes that there would be a total of eighty pupils, it could easily be adapted in line with the basic principles being outlined, whatever the numbers.

Each of these settings, the primary and secondary schools and the FE college, would be carefully selected to ensure that all staff were committed to the integration of pupils with learning difficulties and that there were appropriate classrooms within the main buildings. It would not be appropriate for these units to be placed in a separate classroom block on the other side of the playground.

The staffing ratios in this model are more generous than those currently available in special schools. This is justified in terms of the additional support work needed in mainstream classes to support integrated pupils. The closure of special schools would also provide considerable savings in capital maintenance and overheads which could be used to support these additional staffing levels.

The headteacher, who would carry overall responsibility for the education of all eighty pupils, would probably be based in the secondary school. He/she would have responsibilities for co-ordination and communication across the eight units and with the headteachers and staff in the host schools and would also carry responsibility for liaison with the LEA and other relevant agencies. Clearly, headteachers would have an unusual and demanding role. They would need to co-ordinate scattered and dispersed staff and services, while providing firm leadership and personal and professional support. They would also have responsibility, together with the deputy headteacher, for planning and co-ordinating staff training both for their own special needs staff and for staff in the mainstream school and FE college.

In addition to the in-service training responsibilities referred to above, the deputy head would have a specific leadership function in the secondary school. The two senior teachers would take day-to-day responsibility for co-ordinating the work in each of the two primary schools. Each unit would be headed by a teacher and be supported by two classroom assistants. An additional teacher would be available to support the integration of pupils into mainstream classes.

This model of integration, incorporating headteacher, deputy headteacher, senior teachers and class teachers, as well as classroom assistants, provides a career structure which has been lacking so far in piecemeal attempts at integration.

The amount and nature of integration experienced by each of the pupils would depend on their agreed and assessed needs. Integration would vary along a continuum. For example, pupils with profound and multiple learning difficulties might only experience locational and some social integration. For pupils at the other end of the continuum, full-scale functional integration would be possible for increasing periods of time. Each pupil's need for appropriate locational, social and functional integration would be continuously reviewed.

The establishment of a scheme of this nature would not preclude the neighbourhood integration of some pupils. Staff supporting such pupils could be attached to the staff of the schools outlined in this model in order to avoid professional isolation.

CONCLUSION

Despite methodological problems, the increasing volume of research on the integration of pupils with learning difficulties does suggest that, with careful planning and resourcing and with the commitment of all concerned, pupils with learning difficulties do benefit from increased opportunities to integrate with their mainstream peers. Three possible options for integration have been considered and it is argued that the unit model, described under Option 3, is the one most likely to provide the highest quality education within a mainstream context.

Note: The first part of this chapter is based on an article to be published in the *Journal of Applied Research in Learning Disabilities*, Volume 10 Number 1.

REFERENCES

Aherne, P., Thornber, A., Fagg, S. and Skelton, S. (1990) *Communication for All: A Cross Curricular Skill Involving Interactions Between Speaker and Listener*. London: Fulton.

Ashdown, R., Carpenter, B. and Bovair, K. (eds) (1991) *The Curriculum Challenge: Access to the National Curriculum for Pupils with Learning Difficulties*. London: Falmer Press.

Ashdown, R. (1996) 'Co-ordinating the whole curriculum'. In Carpenter, B., Ashdown, R. and Bovair, K. (eds) *Enabling Access: Effective Teaching and Learning for Pupils with Learning Difficulties*. London: Fulton.

Ainscow, M. and Muncey, J. (1984) *Special Needs Action Programme (SNAP)*. Drake Educational Associates.

Ainscow, M. and Muncey, J. (1989) *Meeting Individual Needs in the Primary School*. London: David Fulton Publishers.

Ainscow, M. and Tweddle, D. A. (1979) *Preventing Classroom Failure: An Objectives Approach*. London: Wiley.

Ainscow, M. and Tweddle, D. A. (1984) *Early Learning Skills Analysis*. London: Wiley.

Ainscow, M. and Tweddle, D. A. (1988) *Encouraging Classroom Success*. London: Wiley.

Balshaw, M. (1991) *Help in the Classroom*. London: Fulton.

Bayliss, P. (1995) 'Integration and interpersonal relations; interactions between disabled children and their non-disabled peers'. *British Journal of Special Education*, 22, 3, 131–140.

Becker, J. A. (1990) 'Process in the Acquisition of Pragmatic Competence'. In G. Conti-Ramsden and C. Snow (eds) *Children's Language, Vol. 7*. London: Erlbaum Associates.

Berger, M. and Yule, W. (1985) 'IQ tests and the assessment of mental handicap'. In Clarke, A.D.B., Clarke, A.M. and Berg, J.M. (eds) *Mental Deficiency: the Changing Outlook*, 4th edition. London: Methuen.

Berger, M. and Yule, W. (1987) 'Psychometric approaches'. In Hogg, J. and Raynes, N. V. *Assessment in Mental Handicap* London: Croom Helm.

Beveridge, S. (1996) 'Experiences of an integration link scheme: the perspectives of pupils with severe learning difficulties and their mainstream peers'. *British Journal of Learning Disabilities*, 24, 1, 9–20.

Billinge, R. (1988) 'The Objectives Model of Curriculum Development: A Creaking Bandwagon?' *Mental Handicap*, 16, 26–29.

Blacher, J. and Turnbull, A. (1982) 'Teacher and parent perspectives on selected social aspects of preschool mainstreaming'. *The Exceptional Child*, 29, 3, 191–199.

Booth, T. (1996) 'A perspective on inclusion from England'. *Cambridge Journal of Education* , 26, 1, 87–101.

Bruner, J. S. (1975) 'The ontegenesis of speech acts'. *The Journal of Child Language*, 2, 1, 1–19.

Burman, L., Farrell, P., Feiler, A., Heffernan. M., Mittler, H. and Reason, R. (1983) 'Redesigning the school curriculum'. *Special Education Forward Trends*, 9, 3, 21–25.

Byers, R. (1994) 'Teaching as Dialogue: Teaching Approaches and Learning Difficulties for Pupils with Learning Difficulties'. In Coupe-O'Kane, J. and Smith, B. (eds) *Taking Control: Enabling People with Learning Difficulties*. London: Fulton.

Byers, R. and Rose, R. (1996) *Planning the Curriculum for Pupils with Special Educational Needs*. London: Fulton.

Byrne, E. A., Cunningham, C. and Sloper, P. (1988) *Families and their Children with Down's Syndrome*. London: Routledge.

Carpenter, B. (1994) 'Shared learning: the developing practice of integration for children with severe learning difficulties'. *European Journal of Special Needs Education*, 9, 2, 182–190.

Carpenter, B. (1996) 'Enabling partnership: families and schools'. In Carpenter, B., Ashdown, R. and Bovair, K. (eds) *Enabling Access: Effective Teaching and Learning for Pupils with Learning Difficulties*. London: Fulton.

Carpenter, B., Ashdown, R. and Bovair, K. (eds) (1996) *Enabling Access: Effective Teaching and Learning for Pupils with Learning Difficulties*. London: Fulton.

Carpenter, B., and Ashdown, R. (1996) 'Enabling access'. In Carpenter, B., Ashdown, R. and Bovair, K. (eds) *Enabling Access: Effective Teaching and Learning for Pupils with* Learning Difficulties. London: Fulton.

Carr, J. and Collins, S. (1992) *Working Towards Independence: A Practical Guide to Teaching People with Learning Disabilities*. London: Jessica Kingsley Publishers.

Carson, S. (1992) 'Joining in at school'. *Learning Together*, 2, 13–14.

Casey, W., Jones, D., Kugler, B. and Watkins, B. (1988) 'Integration of Down's syndrome children in the primary school; a longitudinal study of cognitive development and academic attainments'. *British Journal of Educational Psychology*, 58, 279–286.

Center, Y., Ward, J. and Ferguson, C. (1991) 'Towards an index to evaluate the integration of children with disabilities into regular classes'. *Educational Psychology*, 11, 1, 77–95.

Cole, K. N., Mills, P., Dale, P. S. and Jenkins, J. R. (1992) 'Effects of pre-school integration for children with disabilities'. *Exceptional Children*, 58, 1, 36–44.

Coles, E. and Blunden, R. (1979) 'The Establishment and Maintenance of a Ward-Based Activity Period within a Mental Handicap Hospital'. *Research report No. 8 Cardiff:* Mental Handicap in Wales Applied Research Unit.

Conway, P. and Baker, P. (1996) 'Integration and education: theory and practice'. In Coupe O'Kane, J. and Goldbart, J. (eds) *Whose Choice? Contentious Issues for those Working with People with Learning Difficulties*. London: Fulton.

Coupe, J., Aherne, P., Crawford, N., Herring, J., Jolliffe, J., Levy, D., Malone, J., Murphy, D., Alder, J. and Pott, P. (1987) *Assessment of Early Feeding and Drinking Skills*. Manchester LEA.

Coupe-O'Kane, J. and Baker, M (1993) 'Meeting individual needs through the National Curriculum'. In J. Harris (ed) *Innovations in Educating Children with severe Learning Difficulties*. Lisieux Hall Publishers.

Coupe O'Kane, J. and Smith, B. (1994) (eds) *Taking Control: Enabling People with Learning Difficulties*. London: Fulton.

Coupe-O'Kane, J. and Goldbart, J (eds) (1996) *Whose Choice? Controversial Issues for those Working with People with Learning Difficulties*. London: Fulton.

Cornell, B. and Carden, N. (1990) 'Principles must come first'. *British Journal of Special Education*, 17, 4–7.

Crisp, A. and Sturmey, P. (1988) 'The promotion of purposeful activity in micro-environments for people with a mental handicap'. *American Journal of Mental Deficiency*, 10, 3–5.

CSIE (1989) *The Integration Charter*. Centre for Studies on Inclusive Education.

Cunningham, C. and Davis, H. (1985) *Working with Parents: Frameworks for Collaboration*. Milton Keynes: Open University Press.

DES (1978) 'Special Educational Needs' (The Warnock Report). London: HMSO.

DES/Welsh Office (1985) *The Organisation and Content of the Curriculum: Special Schools (Note)*. London: Department of Education and Science.

DFE (1994a) *Code of Practice on the Identification and Assessment of Special Needs*. London: Department for Education.

DFE (1994b) *Special Educational Needs: A Guide for Parents*. London: Department for Education.

DFE (1994c) *Pupil Behaviour and Discipline: Circular 8/94* Department for Education and Employment Publications Department.

DOH (1993) *Guidance on Permissible Forms of Control in Children's Residential Care*. Department of Health Publications Unit.

Danby, J. and Cullen, C. (1988) 'Integration and mainstreaming: a review of the efficacy of mainstreaming and integration for mentally handicapped pupils'. *Educational Psychology*, 8, 3, 177–195.

Doman, G. (1974) *What to Do about your Brain-injured Child*. London: Cape.

Dunn, L., Dunn, L and Whetton, C. (1982) *The British Picture Vocabulary Scale*. Windsor: NFER-Nelson.

Elliot, C., Murray, J. and Pearson, L. (1983) *British Ability Scales*. Windsor: NFER-Nelson.

Emblem, B. and Conti-Ramsden, G. (1990) 'Towards Level 1: Reality of Illusion?' *British Journal of Special Education*, 17, 3, 88 – 91.

Emerson, E. and McGill, P. (1989a) 'Normalization and applied behavioural analysis'. *Behavioural Psychotherapy*, 17, 101–117.

Emerson, E. and McGill, P. (1989b) 'Normalization and applied behavioural analysis: rapprochement or intellectual imperialism?' *Behavioural Psychotherapy*, 17, 309–313.

Emerson, E. (1992) *What is normalization?* In Brown, H. and Smith, H. (eds) *Normalization: A Reader for the 1990's*. London: Routledge.

Emerson, E. (1995) *Challenging Behaviour: Analysis and Intervention in People with Learning Difficulties*. Cambridge University Press.

Evans, J. (1982) *The Effect on Pupil Engagement of Changing the Seating Arrangements in an SLD Classroom*. Unpublished MSc Thesis, University of Manchester.

Evans, P. (1995) 'Integrating students with special educational needs into mainstream schools in OECD countries'. *Prospects*, 25, 2, 201–219.

Fagg, S., Aherne, P., Skelton, S. and Thornber, A. (1990a) *Entitlement for All in Practice: A broad Balanced and relevant Curriculum for Pupils with Severe and Complex Learning Difficulties in the 1990's*. London: Fulton.

Fagg, S., Skelton, S., Aherne, P. and Thornber, A. (1990b) *Science for All*. London: Fulton.

Farrell, P. (1989) 'Educational psychology services: crisis or opportunity'. *The Psychologist*, 12, 6, 240–241.

References

Farrell, P. (1991) 'Behavioural and interactive teaching for children with severe learning difficulties: match or mismatch?' *Educational and Pupil Psychology*, 8 , 2, 61–69.

Farrell, P. (1992) 'Behavioural methods: a fact of life?' *British Journal of Special Education*, 19, 4, 145–148.

Farrell, P. (1995) 'The impact of normalization policy and provision for people with learning difficulties.' *Issues in Special Education and Rehabilitation*, 10, 1, 47–54.

Farrell, (1995) 'Some reflections on the role of educational psychologists.' In Norwich, B. and Lunt, I. *Psychology and Special Educational Needs: Recent Developments and Future Directions*. Arena: Ashgate Publishing.

Farrell, (1996) 'Integration: where do we go from here?' In Coupe O'Kane, J. and Goldbart, J. (eds) *Whose Choice? Contentious Issues for those Working with People with Learning Difficulties*. London: Fulton.

Farrell, P and Sugden, M. (1985) 'Integrating children with severe learning difficulties: fantasy or reality?' *Education and Child Psychology*, 8, 69–80.

Farrell, P., McBrien, J. and Foxen, T. (1992) *EDY Instructor's Handbook: Second Edition*. Manchester University Press.

Farrell, P., McBrien, J. and Foxen, T. (1993) 'Introducing the second edition of EDY: training staff in behavioural methods.' *Mental Handicap*, 21, 87–91.

Farrell, P. and Scales, A. (1995) 'Who likes to be with whom in an integrated nursery?' *British Journal of Learning Disabilities*, 23, 4, 156–160.

Farrell, P. and Banerjee, R. (1996) *EDY Trainee Workbook: Indian Version*. Calcutta: Indian Institute of Cerebral Palsy.

Fletcher-Campbell, F. (1994) *Still Joining Forces?* Slough: NFER.

Fletcher-Campbell, F. (1996) 'Just another piece of paper? Key Stage 4 accreditation for pupils with learning difficulties.' *British Journal of Special Eduction* , 23, 1, 15–18.

Forlin (1995) 'Educators' Beliefs about inclusive practices in Western Australia.' *British Journal of Special Education*, 22, 4, 179–186.

Foxen, T. and McBrien, J. (1981) *Training Staff in Behavioral Methods: Trainee Workbook*. Manchester University Press.

Foxx, R. M. and Azrin, N. H. (1973) 'The elimination of autistic self stimulatory behaviour by overcorrection.' *Journal of Applied Behavioural Analysis*, 6, 1–14.

Frederickson, N. and Woolfson, H. (1987) 'Integration: the social dimension. *Educational Psychology in Practice*, 3, 2, 42–49.

Gardner, J., Murphy, J. and Crawford, N. (1983) *The Skills Analysis Model: An Effective Curriculum for Children with Severe Learning Difficulties*. Kidderminster: BIMH Publications.

Garner, P., Hinchcliffe, V. and Sandow, S. (1995) *What Teachers Do: Developments in Special Education*. Paul Chapman Publishing.

Garner, P. and Sandow, S. (eds) (1995) *Advocacy and Self Advocacy and Special Needs*. London: Fulton.

Glenn, S. M. and O'Brien, Y. (1994) 'Microcomputers: Do they have a Part to Play in the Education of Children with PMLDs?' In Ware, J. (ed) *Education Pupils with Profound and Multiple Learning difficulties*. London: Fulton.

Gregory, S. P. (1996) 'Inclusive education for preschool children with disabilities.' *Support for Learning*, 11, 2, 77–83.

Grossman, H.J. (ed) 1983) *Classification in Mental Retardation*. American Association on Mental Deficiency, Washington, D.C.

HMI/Audit Commission Report (1992) *Getting in on the Act*. London: HMSO.

Hall, J. (1996) 'Integration, inclusion – what does it all mean?' In Coupe-O'Kane, J. and Goldbart, J. (eds) *Whose Choice? Contentious Issues for those Working with People with Learning Difficulties*. London: Fulton.

Halle, J. H. and Touchette, P. (1987) 'Delayed Prompting: A Method for Instructing Children with Severe Language Handicaps.' In J. Hogg and P. Mittler (eds) *Issues in Staff Training in Mental Handicap*. London: Croom Helm.

Halpin, D. and Lewis, A. (1996) 'The impact of the National Curriculum on twelve special schools in England.' *European Journal of Special Needs Education*, 11, 1, 95–106.

Hanline, M. F. and Halvorsen, A. (1989) 'Parent perceptions of the integration transition process: overcoming artificial barriers.' *Exceptional Children*, 55, 6, 487–492.

Haring, N. G., Liberty, K. A. and White, O. R. (1981) *An Investigation of Phases of Learning and Facilitating Instructional Events for the Severely/Profoundly Handicapped (final project report)*. Seattle: University of Washington College of Education.

Haring, N. G. (ed) (1988) *Generalisation for Students with Severe Handicaps: Strategies and Solutions*. University of Washington Press.

Harris, J. (1988) 'Interactive Styles for Language Facilitation.' In B. Smith (ed) *Interactive Approaches to the Education of Children with Severe Learning Difficulties*. Birmingham: Westhill College.

Harris, J. (1995) 'Responding to pupils with severe learning disabilities who present challenging behaviour.' *British Journal of Special Education*, 222, 3, 109–116.

Harris, J. (1996) 'Physical restraint procedures for managing challenging behaviours presented by mentally retarded children and adults.' *Research in Developmental Disabilities*, 17, 2, 99–134.

Harris, J. C. (1992) 'Neurobiological factors in self-injurious behaviour.' In Luiselli, J. K., Matson, S. L. and Singh, N. N. (eds) *Self Injurious Behaviour: Analysis, Assessment and Treatment*. New York: Springer-Verlag.

Hastings, R. and Graham, S. (1995) 'Adolescents' perceptions of young people with severe learning difficulties: the effects of integration schemes and frequency of contact.' *Educational Psychology*, 15, 2, 149–159.

Hastings, R., Hewes, A., Lock, S. and Witting, A. (1996) 'Do special educational needs courses have any impact on student teachers' perceptions of children with severe learning difficulties?' *British Journal of Special Education*, 23, 3, 139–145.

Hegarty, S. (1987) *Meeting Special Needs in Ordinary Schools*. London: Cassell.

Hegarty, S. (1991) 'Towards an agenda for research in special education.' *European Journal of Special Needs Education*, 6, 2, 87–99.

Hegarty, S. (1993) 'Reviewing the literature on integration.' *European Journal of Special Needs Education*, 8, 3, 194–200.

Heggie, (1994) 'The impact of the National Curriculum on SLD and PMLD pupils.' *The SLD Experience*, 8, 18.

Hogg, J. and Raynes, N. V. (1987) *Assessment in Mental Handicap*. London: Croom Helm.

Hogg, J., Sebba, J. and Lambe, L. (eds) (1990) *Profound Retardation and Multiple Impairment, Volume. 3: Medical and Physical Care and Management*. London: Chapman and Hall.

Hogg, J. and Sebba, J. (1986) *Profound Retardation and Multiple Impairment: Volume 1 – Development and Learning*. London: Croom Helm.

Howlin, P. (1994) 'Special educational treatment.' In Rutter, M., Taylor, E. and Hersov, L. (eds) *Child and Adolescent Psychiatry: Modern Approaches – 3rd Edition*. Oxford: Blackwell.

References

Humphreys, K. (1995) 'Whose reality?' *The SLD Experience*, 12, 4.

Hundert, J. and Houghton, A. (1992) 'Promoting social interaction of children with disabilities in integrated preschools: a failure to generalise.' *Exceptional Children*, 58, 4, 311–320.

ILSMH (1994) *The Delhi Declaration on the Rights and Needs of Persons with Mental Handicap and their Families*. ILSMH: Brussels.

Jeffree, D. and McConkey, R. (1976) *P.I.P. Developmental Charts*. Hodder and Stoughton.

Jeffree, D. and Cheseldine, S. (1982) *Pathways to Independence*. Hodder and Stoughton.

Jenkinson, J. C. (1993) 'Integration of students with severe and multiple learning difficulties.' *European Journal of Special Needs Education*, 8, 3, 320–335.

Jones, G. (1991) *Methods Used by Psychologists to Assess Pre-School Children*. Unpublished MSc Thesis, Department of Education, University of Manchester.

Jones, M. (personal communication) 'Implications of the Children Act for the Education and Care of Children whose Special Needs are Compounded by Severe Challenging Behaviour.'

Jones, M. (1994) 'Including everyone'. *Managing Schools Today*, 36–38.

Jordan, R. and Powell, S. (1994) 'Whose curriculum? Critical notes on integration and entitlement'. *European Journal of Special Needs Education*, 9, 1, 27–39.

Jowett, S., Hegarty, S. and Moses, D. (1988) *Joining Forces*. Windsor: NFER.

Jupp, K. (1992a) 'What are we waiting for?' *Learning Together*, 2, 9–10.

Jupp, K. (1992b) *Everyone Belongs*. London: Souvenir Press.

Jupp, K. (1993) 'The great integration debate: part 1.' *Mental Handicap*, 21, 2, 68–71.

Kiernan, C. (1985) 'The development of communication and cognition.' In Dobbing, J. (ed) *Scientific Studies in Mental Retardation*. Royal Society of Medicine/Macmillan Press.

Kiernan, C. and Qureshi, H. (1993) 'Challenging behaviour.' In Kiernan, C. (ed) *Implications of Research on the Challenging Behaviour of People with Learning Disabilities*. Kidderminster: BILD.

Kiernan, C. and Kiernan, D. (1994) 'Challenging behaviour in schools for pupils with severe learning difficulties.' *Mental Handicap Research*, 7, 117–201.

Lachiewicz, A. M., Spiridigliozzi, G. A., Gullion, C. M., Ransford, S. N. and Rao, K. (1994) 'Aberrant behaviours of young boys with Fragile X syndrome.' *American Journal of Mental Retardation*, 98, 567–579.

Lawson, H. (1992) *Practical Record Keeping for Special Schools*. London: Fulton.

Lewis, A. (1990) 'Integration – a child's eye view'. *Child Education*, No. 34.

Lewis, A. (1993) *Integration in Practice: Learning Difficulties*. University of Birmingham, School of Education; Distance Learning Material.

Lewis, A. (1995) *Children's Understanding of Disability*. London: Routledge.

Lewis, A. (1996) 'Assessment'. In Carpenter, B., Ashdown, R. and Bovair, K. (eds) *Enabling Access: Effective Teaching and Learning for Pupils with Learning Difficulties*. London: Fulton.

Lincoln, J., Batty, J., Townsend, R. and Collins, M. (1992) 'Working for the greater inclusion of children with severe learning difficulties in mainstream secondary schools'. *Educational and Child Psychology*, 9, 4, 46–52.

Lindsay, G. (1989) 'Evaluating integration'. *Educational Psychology in Practice*, 5, 1, 134–143.

Lopez, J. F. G. (1994) 'The integration of mentally retarded children: analysis of an experience in Spain. *European Journal of Special Needs Education*, 9, 1, 145–151.

Lorenz, S. (1992) 'Supporting special needs assistants in mainstream schools'. *Educational and Child Psychology*, 9, 4, 25–34.

Lorenz, S. (1995) 'The placement of pupils with Down's syndrome: a survey of one Northern LEA'. *British Journal of Special Education*, 22, 1, 16–19.

Lowe, M. and Costello, A.J. (1976) *Manual for the Symbolic Play Test*. Windsor: NFER.

Lowe, K. and Felce, D. (1995) 'The definition of challenging behaviour in practice'. *British Journal of Learning Disabilities*, 23, 3, 118–123.

Lubovoski, V. (1988) 'Against integration. *Special Children*, 23, 6–7.

Lyon, C. M. (1994a) *Legal Issues Arising from the Care, Control and Safety of Children with Learning Disabilities who also Present Severe Challenging Behaviour*. London: The Mental Health Foundation.

Lyon, C. M. (1994b) *Legal Issues Arising from the Care and Control of Children with Learning Disabilities who also Present Severe Challenging Behaviour: A Guide for Parents and Carers*. London: The Mental Health Foundation.

McBrien, J. and Weightman, J. (1980) 'The effect of Room Management procedures on the engagement of profoundly retarded children'. *British Journal of Mental Subnormality*, 26, 1, 38–46.

McBrien, J., Farrell, P. and Foxen, T. (1992) *EDY Trainee Workbook: Second Edition*. Manchester University Press.

McBrien, J. and Felce, D. (1994) *Working with People with Severe Learning Difficulty and Challenging Behaviour*. Clevedon: BILD Publications.

McConkey, R. (1985) *Working with Parents: A Practical Guide for Teachers and Therapists*. London: Croom Helm.

McConkey, R. (1988) 'Interaction: The Name of the Game'. In N. Smith (ed) *Interactive Approaches to the Education of Children with Severe Learning Difficulties*. Birmingham: Westhill College.

McConkey, R. (1994) 'An ordinary life for special people'. In Coupe-O'Kane, J. and Smith, B. (eds), *Taking Control: Enabling People with Learning Difficulties*. London: Fulton.

McConkey, R. and Jeffree, R. (1979) 'First steps in learning to pretend'. *Special Education Forward Trends*, 6, 4, 13–18.

McConkey, R. and Jeffree, R. (1980) 'Developing pupils's play'. *Special Education Forward Trends*, 7, 2, 8–12.

McEvoy, J., McDonnell, A. and Dearden, B. (1991) 'Challenging behaviour in the classroom'. *British Journal of Special Education*, 18, 4, 141–144.

McGee, J. J. (1992) 'Gentle teaching's assumptions and paradigm'. *Journal of Applied Behavioural Analysis*, 25, 869–872.

McGee, J. J., Melanoscine, F. J., Hobbs, D. C. and Menousek, P. E. (1987) *Gentle Teaching: A Non-aversive Approach for Helping Persons with Mental Retardation*. New York: Human Sciences Press.

Mace, F. C., Page, T. J., Ivancic, M. T. and O'Brien, S. (1986) 'Analysis of environmental determinants of aggression and disruption in mentally retarded children'. *Applied Research in Mental Retardation*, 7, 203–221.

Madden, N. A. and Slavin, R. F. (1983) 'Mainstreaming students with mild handicaps: academic and social outcomes'. *Review of Educational Research*, 53, 4, 519–589.

Mansell, J., Felce, D., DeKock, V. and Jenkins, J. (1982) 'Increasing purposeful activity of severely and profoundly handicapped adults'. *Behaviour Research and Therapy*, 20, 593–604.

Marks, D., Burman, E., Burman, L. and Parker, I. (1995) 'Collaborative research into education case conferences'. *Educational Psychology in Practice*, 11, 1, 41–49.

References

Martin, G. and Pear, J. (1988) *Behavioural Modification: What it is and how to do it*. Prentice-Hall International.

Matson, J. l., Sadowski, C., Matese, M. and Benavidez, D. (1993) 'Empirical study of mental health professionals' knowledge and attitudes towards the concept of age-appropriateness'. *Mental Retardation*, 31, 5, 340–345.

Mirenda, P. L. and Donnellan, A. M. (1986) 'Effect of adult interactional style on conversational behaviour in students with severe communication problems'. *Language, Speech and Hearing Services in Schools*, 17, 126–141.

Mittler, P. (1991) 'Educating children with severe learning difficulties: challenging vulnerability'. In Tizard, B. (ed) *Vulnerability and Resilience in Human Development*. London: Jessica Kingsley Publishers.

Mittler, P. (1992) *Assessment of People with Mental Retardation*. Geneva: World Health Organisation.

Mittler, P. (1995a) *Person's with Intellectual Disabilities: Changing Perceptions and Demographics*. Opening paper to International Symposium on Intellectual Disability: Programs, Policies and Planning for the Future. United Nations, New York.

Mittler, P. (1995b) 'Rethinking partnership between parents and professionals'. *Children and Society*, 9, 3, 22–40.

Mittler, P. (1996a) 'Laying the foundations for self-advocacy: the role of home and school'. In Coupe-O'Kane, J. and Goldbart, J. (eds) *Whose Choice: Contentious Issues for those working with People with Learning Difficulties*. London: Fulton.

Mittler, P. (1996b) 'Preparing for self-advocacy'. In Carpenter, B., Ashdown, R. and Bovair, K. (eds) *Enabling Access: Effective Teaching and Learning for Pupils with Learning Difficulties*. London: Fulton.

Mittler, P. and McConachie, H. (1983) *Parents, Professionals and Mentally Handicapped People*. London: Croom Helm.

Mittler, P. and Farrell, P. (1987) 'Can children with severe learning difficulties be educated in ordinary schools?' *European Journal of Special Needs Education*, 2, 221–236.

Mittler, P. and Mittler, H. (eds) (1994) *Innovations in Family Support*. Chorley: Lisieux Hall Press.

Moorcroft-Cuckle (1993) 'Type of school attended by children with Down's syndrome. *Educational Research*, 35, 3, 267–9.

Mortimer, H. (1995) 'Welcoming young children with special educational needs into mainstream education'. *Support for Learning*, 10, 4, 164–270.

Mount, H. and Ackerman, D. (1991) *Technology for All*. London: Fulton.

Murphy, G. H. and Oliver, C. (1987) 'Decreasing undesirable behaviours'. In Yule, W. and Carr, J. *Behaviour Modification for People with Mental Handicaps*. London: Croom Helm.

Murphy, G. H., Oliver, C., Corbett, J., Crayton, L., Hales, J., Head, D. and Hall, S. (1993) 'Epidemiology of self injury, characteristics of people with severe self injury and initial treatment outcome'. In Kiernan, C. (ed) *Implications of Research on the Challenging Behaviour of People with Learning Disabilities*. Kidderminster: BILD.

Murphy, G. (1994) 'Services for children and adolescents with severe learning difficulties (mental retardation)'. In Rutter, M., Taylor, E. and Hersov, L. (eds) *Child and Adolescent Psychiatry: Modern Approaches – 3rd Edition*. Oxford: Blackwell.

NCC (1992) *The National Curriculum and Pupils with Severe Learning Difficulties – Curriculum Guidance 9*. York: National Curriculum Council.

NCC (1993) *Special Needs and the National Curriculum: Opportunity and Challenge*. York: National Curriculum Council.

NFER (1995) *Small Steps of Progress in the National Curriculum: An Executive Summary*. Slough: NFER.

Newson, E, (1993) 'Play-based assessment in the special needs classroom'. In Harris, J. (ed) *Innovations in Educating Children with Severe Learning Difficulties*. Chorley: Lisieux Hall Press.

Nind, M. and Hewett, D. (1994) *Access to Communication: Developing the Basics of Communication with People with Severe Learning Difficulties through Intensive Interaction*. London: Fulton.

Nind, M. and Hewett, D. (1996) 'When age-appropriateness isn't age-appropriate'. In Coupe O'Kane, J. and Goldbart, J. (eds) *Whose Choice? Contentious Issues for those Working with People with Learning Difficulties*. London: Fulton.

Nind, M. (1996) 'Efficacy of intensive interaction: developing sociability and communication in people with severe and complex learning difficulties using an approach based on caregiver-infant interaction'. *European Journal of Special Needs Education*, 11, 1, 48–67.

Norgate, R. (1994) 'Responding to the challenge: planning for the needs of children with severe learning difficulties who present challenging behaviour'. *Educational Psychology in Practice*, 9, 4, 201–207.

Norwich, B. (1992) *The National Curriculum and Special Educational Needs*. Bedford Way Paper: University of London Institute of Education.

Nyhan, W. L. (1994) 'The Lesch-Nyhan disease'. In Thompson, T. and Gray, D. B. (eds) *Destructive Behaviour in Developmental Disabilities: Diagnosis and Treatment*. Sage: Thousand Oaks.

OECD/CERI (1992) *Integration in the School: Reports of Case Studies Undertaken in the UK*. Slough: NFER.

O'Brien, J. (1987) 'A guide to lifestyle planning: using the Activities catalogue to integrate services and natural support systems'. In Wilcox, B.W. and Bellamy, G.T. (eds) *The Activities Catalogue: An Alternative Curriculum for Youth and Adults with Severe Disabilities*. Brookes: Baltimore.

O'Connell, R. (1994) 'Proving integration works: how effective is the integration of students with PMLDs into the mainstream of an SLD school in increasing their opportunities for social integration?' In Ware, J. (ed) *Educating Children with Profound and Multiple Learning Difficulties*. London: Fulton.

Oliver, C., Murphy, G. H. and Corbett, J. A. (1987) 'Self-injurious behaviour in people with mental handicap: a total population survey'. *Journal of Mental Deficiency Research*, 31, 147–162.

Ouvry, C. (1994) 'The great integration debate: part 4'. *British Journal of Learning Disabilities*, 22, 1, 27–30.

Pary, R. (1993) 'Psychoactive drugs used with adults and elderly adults who have mental retardation'. *American Journal of Mental Retardation*, 98, 121–127.

Pedlar, A. (1990) 'Normalization and integration: a look at the Swedish experience'. *Mental Retardation*, 28, 5, 275–281.

Phillips, V. and McCullough, L. (1990) 'Consultation based programming: instituting a collaborative ethic in schools'. *Exceptional Children*, 45, 291–304.

Philps, E. (1994) *A Comparative Study of the Academic Achievement and Language Development of Children with Down's Syndrome Placed in Mainstream and Special Schools*. Unpublished MPhil Thesis, Department of Educational Research, University of Wolverhampton.

Pope, C. (1988) 'Room Management with target setting in a classroom for pupils with severe mental handicaps'. *Mental Handicap Research*, 1, 186–196.

Porter, J. (1996) 'Issues in teacher training. In Carpenter, B., Ashdown, R. and Bovair, K. (eds) *Enabling Access: Effective Teaching and Learning for Pupils with Learning Difficulties*. London: Fulton.

Porter, J., Grove, N. and Park, K. (1996) 'Ages and stages: what is appropriate behaviour?' In Coupe-O'Kane, J. and Goldbart, J (eds) (1996) *Whose Choice? Controversial Issues for those Working with People with Learning Difficulties*. London: Fulton.

Porterfield, J., Blunden, R. and Blewitt, E. (1977) *Improving environments for profoundly handicapped adults: establishing staff routines for high client engagement*. Research Report, Mental Handicap in Wales: Applied Research Unit, University of Wales, Cardiff.

Presland, J. (1991) 'Problem behaviours and people with profound and multiple handicaps'. *Mental Handicap*, 19, 66–72.

Pyke, N. (1990) 'Protect staff or we prosecute'. *The Times Educational Supplement*, 30.11.90.

Raybould, E. C. and Solity, J. E. (1988a) 'Precision Teaching . . . and all that! *British Journal of Special Education*, 15, 1, 32–33.

Raybould, E. C. and Solity, J. E. (1988b) 'More Questions on precision Teaching. *British Journal of Special Education*, 15, 2, 59–61.

Rectory Paddock School Staff (1983) *In Search of a Curriculum*. Sidcup: Robin Wren Publications.

Remington, R. (ed) (1991) *The Challenge of Severe Mental Handicap: A Behaviour Analytic Approach*. Chichester: Wiley.

Robertson, J., Emerson, E., Mason, H., Mason, L., Fowler, S., Letchford, S. and Jones, M. (1996) 'Behavioural residential special education for children with severely challenging behaviours: the views of parents'. *British Journal of Special Education*, 23, 2, 80–89.

Rose, R. (1991) 'A jigsaw approach to group work'. *British Journal of Special Education*, 18, 2, 54–57.

Rose, R., Fergusson, A., Coles, C., Byers, R. and Banes, D. (1994) *Implementing the Whole Curriculum for Pupils with Learning Difficulties*. London: Fulton.

Rouse, M. and Florian, L. (1996) 'Effective inclusive schools: a study in two countries'. *Cambridge Journal of Education*, 26, 1, 71–87.

Rutter, M., Maughan, B., Mortimore, P. and Ouston, J. (1979) *Fifteen Thousand Hours: Secondary Schools and their Effects on Children*. London: Open Books.

SCAA (1996) *Planning the Curriculum for Pupils with Profound and Multiple Learning Difficulties*. London: SCAA.

Sainato, D., Goldstein, H. and Strain, P. (1992) 'Effects of self-evaluation on pre school children's use of social interaction strategies with their classmates with autism'. *Journal of Applied Behavioural Analysis*, 7, 475–500.

Scales, A. (1993) *Friendship Patterns in Integrated Nursery Provision for Children with Severe Learning Difficulties and Resulting Attitudes of Mainstream Students*. Unpublished Dissertation, Department of Education, University of Manchester.

Schaffer, H. R. (ed) (1977) *Studies in Mother-Infant Interaction*. London: Academic Press.

Sebba, J. and Clarke, J. (1991) 'Meeting the needs of pupils in history and geography'. In Ashdown, R., Carpenter, B. and Bovair, K. (eds) *The Curriculum Challenge: Pupils with Severe Learning Difficulties and the National Curriculum*. London: Falmer Press.

Sebba, J. and Byers, R. (1992) 'The National Curriculum: control or liberation for pupils with learning difficulties'. *The Curriculum Journal*, 3, 1, 143–160.

Sebba, J., Byers, R. and Rose, R. (1995) *Redefining the Whole Curriculum for Pupils with Learning Difficulties*. London: Fulton.

Sebba, J. and Ainscow, M. (eds) (1996a) 'International Developments in Inclusive Education'. *Cambridge Journal of Education – Special Issue*, 26, 1.

Sebba, J. and Ainscow, M. (1996b) 'International developments in inclusive education – mapping the issues'. *Cambridge Journal of Education*, 26, 1, 5–19.

Segal, S. (1993) 'The great integration debate: Part 2'. *Mental Handicap*, 21, 109–111.

Selfe, L. (1993) 'A review of legislation and classification relating to children with special needs'. In Harris, J. (ed) *Innovations in Educating Children with Severe Learning Difficulties*. Chorley: Lisieux Hall Press.

SENTC (1996) *Professional Development to Meet Special Educational Needs: Report to the Department of Education and Employment*. Flash Ley Resource Centre, Hawksmoor Road, Stafford.

Slavin, R. (1987) *Co-operative Learning*. Washington D.C.: National Educational Association.

Slee, R. (1991) 'Learning initiatives to include all children in regular schools'. In Ainscow, M. (ed) *Effective Schools for All*. London: Fulton.

Smith, B. (ed) (1988) *Interactive Approaches to the Education of Children with Severe Learning Difficulties*. Birmingham: Westhill College.

Smith, B. (ed) (1991) *Interactive Approaches to Teaching the Core Subjects*. Bristol: Lame Duck Publishing.

Smith, B. (1994) 'Handing over control to people with learning difficulties'. In Coupe-O'Kane, J. and Smith, B. (eds) *Taking Control: Enabling People with Learning Difficulties*. London: Fulton.

Smith, B. (1996) 'Discussion: Age-appropriate or developmentally appropriate activities?' In Coupe-O'Kane, J. and Goldbart, J. (eds), *Whose Choice? Controversial Issues for those Working with People with Learning Difficulties*. London: Fulton.

Spencer, R. (1993) *The Inservice Needs of Staff Involved in the Integration of Children with Severe Learning Difficulties*. Unpublished MSc Thesis, Department of Education, University of Manchester.

Stainback, S., Stainback, W. and East, K. (1994) 'A commentary on inclusion and the development of a positive self-identity by people with disabilities'. *Exceptional Children*, 60, 6, 486–490.

Steele, J. and Mitchell, D. (1992) 'Special links with mainstream'. *Special Children*, 14–16.

Stenfert-Kroese, B. and Fleming, I. (1993) 'Prevalence and persistency of challenging behaviour in children'. In Fleming, I. and Stenfert-Kroese, B. (ed) *People with Learning Disability and Severe Challenging Behaviour: New Developments in Services and Therapy*. Manchester University Press.

Stobart, G. (1986) 'Is integrating the handicapped psychologically defensible?' *Bulletin of the British Psychological Society*, 39, 1–4.

Sturmey, P. and Crisp, A. (1989) 'Organising staff to provide individual teaching in a group: A critical review of Room Management and other related procedures'. *Australia and New Zealand Journal of Developmental Disabilities*, 15, 2, 127–124.

Stutsman, R. (1931) *Guide for Administering the Merrill Palmer Scales of Mental Tests*. Chicago: Stoelting.

Thomas, G. (1992) *Effective Classroom Teamwork: Support or Consultation*. London: Routledge.

Thomas, M. (1985) 'Introduction to Classroom Management'. In P. Farrell (ed) *EDY: Its impact on Staff Training in Mental Handicap*. Manchester University Press.

References

Tilstone, T. (1991) *Teaching Children with Severe Learning Difficulties: Practical Approaches*. London: Fulton.

Times Educational Supplement (1992) 'Secure in a special school without its own front door'. *TES*, May 1st.

Toon, C. (1988) 'Integrating children with severe learning difficulties into mainstream schools'. *Education in the North*, 24, 42–52.

Tyne, A. (1993) 'The great integration debate: part 3'. *Mental Handicap*, 21, 4, 150–152.

United Nations (1993) *The Rights of the Child*. Department of Health; Children's Rights Development Unit.

Vizziello, G. F., Bet, M. and Sandona, G. (1994) 'How classmates interact with an autistic child in a mainstream class'. *European Journal of Special Needs Education*, 9, 1, 246–260.

Ward, J., Center, Y. and Bochner, S. (1994) 'A question of attitudes: integrating children with disabilities into regular classrooms'. *British Journal of Special Education*, 21, 1, 34–39.

Ware, J. (1994a) 'Implementing the 1988 Act with pupils with PMLDs'. In Ware, J. (ed) *Educating Children with Profound and Multiple Learning Difficulties*. London: Fulton.

Ware, J. (1994b) 'Classroom organisation'. In Ware, J. (ed) *Educating Children with Profound and Multiple Learning Difficulties*. London: Fulton.

Ware, J. and Evans, P. (1987) 'Room Management is not enough?' *British Journal of Special Education*, 14, 2, 78–80.

Ware, J., Sharman, M., O'Connor, S. and Anderson, M. (1992) 'Interactions between pupils with severe learning difficulties and the mainstream peers'. *British Journal of Special Education*, 19, 4, 153–158.

Wechsler, D. (1992) *Wechsler Intelligence Scale for Children – Third Edition (UK)*. The Psychological Corporation: Harcourt, Brace & Company.

Westwood, P. (1993) *Commonsense Methods for Children with Special Needs (2nd. ed.)*. London: Routledge.

White, M. and Cameron, S. (1987) *Portage Early Education Programme*. Windsor: NFER-Nelson.

Whittaker, J. (1992) 'Can anyone help me to understand the logic of Snoezelen?' *Learning Together*, 2, 23–24.

Whittaker, P. (1994) 'Mainstream students talk about integration'. *British Journal of Special Education*, 21, 1, 13–16.

WHO (1968) *Organisation of Services for the Mentally Retarded, Fifteenth Report of the WHO Expert Committee on Mental Health, WHO Technical Report*. Serial 392, Geneva: World Health Organisation.

Winup, K. (1994) 'The role of a student committee in promotion of independence among school leavers'. In Coupe-O'Kane, J. and Smith, B. (eds) (1994) *Taking Control: Enabling People with Learning Difficulties*. London: Fulton.

Wolfensberger, W. (1972) *The Principle of Normalization in Human Services*. Toronto: National Institute on Mental Retardation.

Wolfensberger, W. (1983) 'Social Role Valorisation: a proposed new term for the principle of normalization'. *Mental Retardation*, 21, 6, 235–239.

Wolkind, S. (1992) 'The Children Act: a cynical view from an ivory tower. *Association of Child Psychology and Psychiatry Review and Newsletter*, 15, 1, 40–41.

Wyton, H. (1993) *The Functional Integration of Children with Severe Learning Difficulties*. Unpublished MSc Thesis, Department of Education, University of Manchester.

Zarkowska, E. and Clements, J. (1994) *Problem Behaviour and People with Severe Learning Disabilities: The STAR Approach*. London: Chapman and Hall.

Zigler, E., Hodapp, R. M. and Edison, M. R. (1990) 'From theory to practice in the care and education of mentally retarded individuals'. *American Journal of Mental Retardation*, 95, 1, 1–12.

INDEX OF AUTHORS CITED

Subject Index